"Honest. Powerful. Compassionate. Practical. Needed... are the words that came to mind when reading Crystal Renaud's book *Dirty Girls Come Clean*. A great challenge for women of all ages to come clean!"

CRAIG GROSS
Founder of XXXchurch.com and author of *Eyes of Integrity*

"I appreciate Crystal Renaud's honesty and courage in sharing her own struggles with a rarely discussed issue among women. By shedding light on this, she will no doubt help many women out of darkness and isolation."

LARISSA LAM
JCTV Host

"Thanks to *Dirty Girls Come Clean*, Christian women now have a voice that describes their secret struggle with pornography. In this hope-filled volume, Crystal outlines a realistic process for 'coming clean' and helps women take those important first steps toward freedom."

MARNIE C. FERREE, MA, LMFT
Executive and Clinical Director of Bethesda Workshops; author of *No Stones—Women Redeemed from Sexual Addiction* and L.I.F.E. Guide for Women.

"*Dirty Girls Come Clean* is an excellent resource for women about the topic of sex, desire, and pornography. With story, honesty, hope, and lots of grace, Crystal Renaud takes this sensitive topic, one that often leads women toward guilt-filled dead ends, and reveals pathways toward forgiveness and healing."

MATTHEW PAUL TURNER
Author of *Churched* and *Hear No Evil*

"Crystal's voice is unmistakably clear in a culture void of healing, comfort, and hope for the broken. If you are that girl, this book is for you."

RENEE JOHNSON
Speaker and author, www.devotionaldiva.com

"The most powerful thing about *Dirty Girls Come Clean* is that Crystal goes first. Her willingness to openly share her struggles and road to sobriety creates a safe place for others to come clean. This book is so engaging and practical that I wouldn't be surprised if both women and men are deeply impacted by reading it."

DAVID TROTTER
Author and speaker—LAUNCH52.com

"Crystal tackles the taboo subject of pornography addiction and bares her soul in her courageous confessional of her own struggle with it. The testimonies of women in this book display hope and will profoundly inspire you. *Dirty Girls Come Clean* will give you a taste of freedom and you will see just how contagious that is."

CINDY BEALL
Author of *Healing Your Marriage When Trust Is Broken*

"We've heard a lot about men and pornography, but precious little from women who struggle with porn addiction. If the adage 'you're only as sick as your secrets' is true, then Crystal Renaud's book will help a lot of women get out of their shame and secrecy and into the light of confession and healing."

SUSAN ISAACS
Actress and author of *Angry Conversations with God*

"*Dirty Girls Come Clean* is an honest, thoughtful and poignant treatment. The stories are a reminder to us that sexual temptations are not just a 'guy' thing. It honors the different ways in which women enter into struggles with sexual issues. *Dirty Girls* will be shocking to some, but the hope within it makes it a must read for those who want to take these issues head on."

WILLIAM M. STRUTHERS, PHD
Associate Professor of Psychology, Wheaton College
Author of *Wired for Intimacy*

"You're not alone. None of us are. *Dirty Girls Come Clean* is a must-read for all teenage girls as well as parents of teenage girls. Porn addiction for women is only a taboo subject because we've made it that way. It's time to start talking and take away the hold it has over us."

JENNI CLAYVILLE
Worship and Creative Leader
Blogger at JenniClayville.com

CRYSTAL RENAUD

MOODY PUBLISHERS

CHICAGO

Edited by Pam Pugh
Interior Design: Ragont Design
Cover Design: Design by Julia
Cover Image: iStock photo / Jim Jurica

Library of Congress Cataloging-in-Publication Data
Renaud, Crystal.
   Dirty girls come clean / Crystal Renaud.
   p. cm.
   Includes bibliographical references.
   ISBN 978-0-8024-6300-5
   1. Pornography—-Religious aspects—-Christianity. 2. Christian women—Religious life. 3. Chastity. I. Title.
   BV4597.6.R46 2011
   241'.667082—dc22

                  2010048873

We hope you enjoy this book from Moody Publishers. Our goal is to provide high-quality, thought-provoking books and products that connect truth to your real needs and challenges. For more information on other books and products written and produced from a biblical perspective, go to www.moodypublishers.com or write to:

Moody Publishers
820 N. LaSalle Boulevard
Chicago, IL 60610

1 3 5 7 9 10 8 6 4 2

Printed in the United States of America

To Dana (DeMoss) Bowman for being so much more than just a teacher, but a friend to a shy girl who needed one. And for helping me find my voice through the written word. For all those years ago and your friendship today, I'm so very thankful for you.

Contents

FOREWORD

Anne Jackson

I thought I was the only one.

As a sixteen-year-old girl, a combination of curiosity and hormones was the catalyst to me typing in three little letters on my family's computer that would forever change my life. S - E - X.

I pressed enter and the images, videos, and chat rooms took full control over the pixels on the computer screen and eventually, my life.

I was hurting from an emotionally absent father, moving hundreds of miles away from my best friends, and an abusive relationship with a youth pastor ten years my senior. Internet pornography became medicine for the empty feelings of worthlessness that so often haunted me in my late teens.

I moved out when I was seventeen, and my habit of looking at porn online only escalated. Soon, I'd be calling sex phone lines. And then I'd watch videos with friends. Everything I saw showed me that to be loved you needed to give sex. To be considered beautiful, you had to be naked. My online habits turned offline and I began meeting with random men and becoming physically involved with them. To this date, I couldn't tell you any of their names or anything about them.

My addiction to pornography and to "love" (please note the quotation marks—what I was doing with these men was certainly not love by any definition) was taking over my life. When I woke up from another random encounter half-dressed and fully clueless of where I was or what had happened, I realized something had to be done. I dressed myself, drove home, and took my computer to the Dumpster outside of my apartment.

I walked back up the stairs and closed the door. For the first time in a very long time, I prayed to a God I wasn't even sure existed anymore and begged Him to forgive me for all of the shameful things I did. Surely that confession was good enough and would remove the weight of the secrets I had been carrying for years.

Nobody knew I looked at porn. After all, I was a girl. I thought I was the only one.

Three years later, the shame and weight of my addiction (even though I had been sober for quite some time) was becoming too much to bear. I tearfully told a sweet girl named Kristi about all of the terrible things that colored my past. She held me as I cried, and helped me stay sober. She was my support, my accountability, and the only person who knew my story.

And then, three years after I told Kristi, at a high school rock show, I felt I needed to share my story with someone else. There was an eighteen-year-old girl named Crystal— quirky and shy— sitting alone at a table. I joined her and begged God for wisdom on how to tell her my story. Why? I could see deep down through her gentle spirit that she was carrying the same weight I had carried for years. Crystal was addicted to porn.

In between bands, I told her about my addiction and asked for her help. At first, she seemed shocked. I was embarrassed for putting her in an awkward position . . . I mean, I didn't know her very well and now she knew something about me that almost nobody knew. The next band took the stage, and after they finished, she turned around to me, tears in her eyes, and confessed her addiction in a flurry of emotion and pain and shame.

She was addicted to porn. And she thought she was the only one.

After confessing, the weight I saw earlier that night lifted. She was now breathing air not polluted by the shame she had been carrying.

As the years have passed and as my story has been shared, that's the comment I keep hearing . . .

"I thought I was the only one."

I'm here to tell you you're not.

And now, several years after that confession at a rock show, Crystal is here to tell you you're not alone.

You see, both of us have walked down this road. Both of us have found help and hope.

Crystal has a unique call on her life to share honestly the dark corners of her past so that you can see how light has entered and redeemed what she considered a lost cause.

Maybe you feel that way now. You feel alone and that there is no possible way you will ever be free from this addiction.

You are not alone, and you can be free.

Read Crystal's words with an open heart. Let the pain and freedom she's experienced flow into your own story.

Again, you are not alone. And you can be free.

Please let this book help you.

It's hard work, but it's more than worth it in the end.

ANNE JACKSON
Author, *Permission to Speak Freely:*
Essays and Art on Fear, Confession, and Grace
AnneJacksonWrites.com

WALK AWAY

—or Jump In

It began with frustration.

I had been leading pornography addiction recovery groups for women for about a year when it came to the point that I needed something more from the material I was using. It was great material.

In fact, it was powerful material.

But it was written for female sex addicts. Largely written for and focused on women recovering from promiscuity, adultery, sexual abuse, and more. Women who struggle with pornography were only mentioned here and there. It contained no real-life accounts of women who had been down this road before and revealed very little about the problem or how to be released from its hold.

As if pornography and pornography-related behavior couldn't be all a woman struggled with. As if she had to be wholly sexually aggressive. As if she had to have larger issues because she was using and viewing pornography.

Women were beginning to tell me, "Hey, this book really isn't for me."

Not entirely true. But I could see their point.

While pornography and pornography-related behavior are definitely sexual addictions, these women had a hard time seeing themselves as full-blown sex addicts. They were becoming resistant to the process of recovery because of this label.

So I searched high and low for Christ-centered material that focused less on whole sexual addiction and more on a woman's use of and addiction to pornography. One that walked through what leading a woman through recovery is supposed to look like.

Unfortunately I turned up empty-handed.

Were there really no recovery books for women with pornography addiction? There were a few books on the topic of pornography addiction for men, and there were many more for wives with addicted husbands.

But nowhere could I find a single recovery resource on the effects of pornography addiction in women or any substantial information on how to specifically help them overcome it.

And that's when I felt it.

Standing in the middle of a Christian bookstore (choking on the smell of Christmas potpourri), feeling defeated and frustrated at the deadend I'd found myself in, I felt God's impression to write this book.

I immediately sent my friend a text message, letting her in on this absurd book-writing idea.

"I think I am supposed to write a book about female pornography addiction."

Her response: "Of course you are."

When God first laid it on my heart to begin sharing my story and minister to women addicted to pornography, I never in my wildest imagination thought He'd ask me to write a book. After all, I was only leading a humble group of women in my local church. If I am being honest, there were only three women attending my group at the time.

Expose my own addiction story for hundreds, perhaps even thousands of people to eventually read?

That's humorous, God.

But that's exactly what He directed me to do.

In February of 2009, I launched the website DirtyGirlsMinistries.com to host surveys specifically for women who were in addiction to pornography or who at one time struggled in the area of pornography addiction. Following in the footsteps of a friend who had written a book several months prior, I knew that in order to get a solid foundation for writing, I needed the data these surveys would provide. I needed to see with new eyes, beyond what my own eyes had already seen, just how widespread the porn problem among women really was.

In less than one week, I received over 300 survey responses

and countless e-mails from women all around the world.

All revealing about themselves something they likely had never revealed before.

I knew about my own addiction. I knew about my accountability partner's addiction. And while there were similarities in our two stories, these surveys proved above all else that there was no formula. There was no pattern or single common denominator for how or why a woman would become addicted to pornography.

These women were young. These women were old. These women were married. These women were single. They were mothers. And daughters. And sisters. And wives. And some of them were even in ministry.

The only things these women had in common were that they each had a name, they were someone's someone, and they were living secret lives of pornography addiction. And they all fully believed they were the only women who did.

Throughout this book, I will come clean about my own eight-year battle with pornography addiction and how I was ultimately set free from it.

You will also read the stories of several other brave women who will come clean. Real women just like you, who found freedom from their addiction in similar ways as I did and allowed me to use their stories as hope for you. Pornography had profoundly affected the lives of these women—by choice and otherwise.

This book is not for sensationalism's sake or to be something I am praised for writing. This book is a testament to the bravery of the women who stepped up to complete a survey and the women therein who shared their stories with me. It is because of these women, and the women who will read this book with hope in their hearts and a relentless call by God, that this book has now come to fruition.

And this book is for you, the woman who feels alone in addiction to pornography. I don't believe in coincidences. This book is in your hands because God wants to speak some truth to you, and, for whatever reason, He's chosen to use this book to do so.

The dark cloud of this addiction is far-reaching. Pornography addiction knows no path other than one of destruction, isolation, and suffocation. Pornography addiction knows no creed. Pornography addiction knows no gender.

We are all sexual beings. If not, you and I would not be living on this earth. So to believe that pornography can only be a man's problem is not only false, but it is an ignorant lie that comes from the enemy.

The enemy, Satan, deceived Eve in the garden of Eden by convincing her that if she ate the forbidden fruit, she would be like God. She in turn offered Adam the fruit, he took some, and as a result of their disobedience, they were expelled from the beautiful garden where they had enjoyed perfect fellowship with God. Satan's goal was to destroy. And the enemy has been trying to destroy women ever since.

From the first bite of a piece of forbidden fruit to pornography addiction, the enemy will use whatever he can to deceive us and keep us ineffective for use in the kingdom of God.

May you find comfort in knowing that not only are you not alone in your struggle, but there is hope for breaking the stronghold of this addiction.

And that hope comes from Jesus.

I write this book from a Christian point of view because it is my personal belief that Jesus is the reason I stand free from pornography today. But as I said, pornography addiction knows no creed. Pornography affects everyone. So it is my hope that the steps provided throughout this book will be beneficial to all women, from all walks of life.

You were created for so much more than this life you've been living. Life is to be lived abundantly. It is time to come on out from behind the bushes.

Life is waiting.

Testimonial:

Crystal: I'll Come Clean First

It was an ordinary day.

I had just arrived home from another long day in the sixth grade and made myself a big glass of milk mixed with a little chocolate syrup. A staple around my house. Leaving my homework for later (or never), I headed to the couch to watch TV.

But on the way there, I took a brief detour to the bathroom.

What I would discover there and the events that followed on that crisp autumn afternoon would soon change the course of my entire life.

Hi, I'm Crystal ... and for eight years I battled a pornography addiction.

How's that for getting right to the point?

I know that if I don't begin straight away by telling you my story, you'll look at me and look at this book as just another self-help by someone who doesn't have a clue.

But hear this sweet sister:

I'm a woman who has been where you are.

I'm a woman who has endured countless church sermons describing only men's struggle with pornography addiction.

I am a woman who knows what it is like to be in a women's Bible study and have the group leader pass right over any chapters that deal with lust because "no one here has an issue with that."

I am a woman who knows that you have likely made attempts to free your life of pornography.

I am a woman who knows you have likely failed miserably at those attempts and more times than you'd care to admit.

I am a woman who knows that you likely feel like the only woman to ever struggle with this addiction.

The truth is, the number of women addicted to pornography is growing rapidly every single day.

The statistics are staggering. But not surprising.

Here are just a few of those statistics. These are from back in 2003 so one can only assume the numbers have increased, not decreased with the rapid growth of Internet use.

- Breakdown of male/female visitors to pornography sites: 72 percent male and 28 percent female.
- 70 percent of women keep their cyber activities secret.
- 17 percent of all women struggle with pornography addiction.
- Women favor chat rooms two times more than men.
- 1 of 3 visitors to all adult websites are women.
- 9.4 million women access adult websites each month.
- 13 percent of all women admitted to accessing pornography while at work.
- Women, far more than men, are likely to act out their behaviors in real life, such as having multiple partners, casual sex, or affairs.[1]

You're thinking statistics are just numbers. What does it mean about you personally? Or what do I, the author of this book, personally know about pornography addiction?

More than I care to mention actually. But I will.

My rendezvous with pornography began in October of 1996. Just a month short of my eleventh birthday. That's right, I was only ten years old when I first stumbled upon pornography.

Here's another stat . . . the average age a child first sees pornography is age eleven.[2]

In the summer of 1996, we had just moved because my dad's job transferred us from Minnesota to Kansas. My mom, recovering from a two-year stint of clinical depression, had to start working out side the home. My dad was away on business trips more than he was home.

My brothers, although older, lacked the interest or maturity to take good care of me. As their nosy little sister, I knew a great deal about what they were going through. I even did my best to help keep them out of trouble.

I enjoyed a peaceful home. Even when it was sometimes only peaceful because I worked hard to keep it that way. I was always the peacemaker. I never wanted my brothers to even get grounded . . . or kicked out. And, given what they were doing, that could have been a possibility.

So almost daily, I came home from school to an empty house. It never bothered me, though. In fact, I relished my solitude.

I had my routine.

Drop my book bag on the floor. Check.

Grab a snack and a drink from the fridge. Check.

Locate seat impression left on the couch from the day before. Check.

Even though my mom had her struggles with depression off and on when I was a kid, she remained very protective.

My dad was pretty checked-out faithwise as he was a nonpracticing Catholic who stopped going to church completely by the time I was eight years old. My mom, however, was a woman of great Christian conviction.

And I mean conviction.

Being that I was a child of the eighties, my mom followed the rules for being a "good Christian mom" at that time, which meant we didn't go trick-or-treating, didn't believe in Santa Claus or the Easter Bunny, and didn't even watch *The Smurfs*.

Even going as far as putting in place adult content blocks on our cable box and Internet filtering (when the Internet came of age in my high school years).

Some would say she went overboard.

Needless to say, she kept me safe back then. Naïve.

But no filter, password, or accountability software could have protected me from what my oldest brother had brought into our home.

So on that nothing-out-of-the-ordinary afternoon when I found a certain questionable magazine sitting in our downstairs bathroom . . . I was taken aback.

Sure, I had seen romantic movies. Perhaps even a naked woman on film when my mom couldn't cover my eyes quickly enough. But I had no idea what sex actually was.

22

Let alone have even a clue what pornography was.

It was because of my naïve nature, this heightened curiosity, and the neglect of being home alone at such a young age that I decided to explore my newfound discovery.

I picked up the magazine. I opened the front cover. And it happened.

In that one moment, in less than a second's time, I not only exposed my eyes to a concept I had never seen before, but I exposed my heart, my mind, and my body to a world that no ten-year-old should ever have entered.

Counselors (to this day I love counseling) I've had over the years have compared the emotional trauma this first exposure to pornography caused me to the emotional trauma of a rape victim.

While that was a difficult parallel for me to accept because I have known women who have been physically raped, it was true.

It was true because of how I reacted to that initial experience.

Reality was that I came in contact with pornography completely innocently. But the reality I believed was the amount of shame I felt and amount of blame I placed on myself for even looking at it in the first place.

And on some level it began to complete me.

Especially since my use of pornography didn't stop with that one magazine, but became the catalyst for what would be a long, painful road ahead.

I soon (and rather quickly) discovered that pornography was everywhere. And it was easily accessible virtually anywhere I went.

Leaving absolutely no stone unturned, I engaged in pornography on television, in movies, and eventually on the Internet.

As I got a little bit older (around my mid-teens), my pornography watching turned into more than just looking when I began to masturbate as part of a regular routine.

And the best part about it was, I could get my physical and emotional needs met while still carrying around my V card.

Because ironically, being a virgin and being known for my virtue was really important to me. I knew that my brothers were not sexually pure. I remember them sneaking girls into their rooms really late at night from the time I was eleven or twelve years old. My dad wasn't around to know, and my mom was often in bed well before their late-night escapades began.

However, I knew how important purity was to my mom, and I didn't want to become known as the weirdo girl who loved pornography.

So in my sin, I became a deceiver. As with most addicts, I covered my tracks well.

Ask anyone who was in my life at that time, and they would tell you they had no clue I was engaged in such a battle.

When I finally told my mom about my addiction many years later, I did so in layers so as not to totally throw her into a coma.

She was clueless. Everyone had been clueless.

I was involved in all of the right activities and kept my grades up. I was clearly the poster child of good behavior.

And I used that reputation to my advantage.

In fact, my reputation was so good that the one time when I was caught viewing pornography, I came away unscathed.

In tenth grade I was viewing adult content on a classroom computer after school. I accidentally printed a page of this content to the library. The librarian of course found it on the printer before I could get there to intercept it. He called me to the library to ask me about it (my user ID printed on the page).

The result of our meeting was that I somehow lied my way out of some serious trouble. How or why he believed me still baffles me. But it just goes to show how deceptive I had become.

The thing about living a life of deception, though, is that it promotes a life of isolation as well.

I was too ashamed to tell anyone about what I was doing. It was bad enough that I was struggling with this, but adding on the fact that I was a girl? No way could I let anyone in on that. In my mind I was the only girl who ever struggled with a pornography and sexual addiction.

I was also fearful that if anyone found out, they'd make me stop. And frankly, that was not something I was willing to do. Yet.

So I kept relationships shallow and people at a distance.

Pornography became my closest friend. My only friend.

Pornography was a friend like none I had ever had before. Consistent. Reliable.

And on some level, incredibly satisfying.

A friend that provided me comfort and security, both emotionally and physically.

And I took my friend almost everywhere.

Just like alcohol or drugs, pornography stimulates hormones

our body can begin to crave. We can even begin to believe we need it.

I can't speak for every woman, but what I found in my research surveys and what was definitely true in my own life is that, unlike for men, the addiction to pornography in women is not as much about how it makes her feel physically, but how it meets her emotional needs.

Women are designed by God to need emotional intimacy.

In my own life, pornography and the behaviors pornography led me to filled a huge need for intimacy, affection, and acceptance.

A need for intimacy that I should have sought Christ to receive.

The relationship a girl has with her dad is crucial to her emotional and spiritual development.

A girl should hear from her dad from a very early age how very beautiful she is.

How delighted in her he is.

How much he loves her.

Because women will often see

Pornography use took me places I never thought I would go. It kept me there longer than I intended to stay. And it cost me more than I wanted to pay.

their heavenly Father in the same way they see their earthly father. And if what she finds from her dad is rejection, abandonment, or perhaps even cruelty, then she will believe God is the same way.

We paint the face of God with the face of our dads, our moms, or even our abusers. And those faces become our theology and mandate how we respond to Him when faced with difficulty. Or perhaps our lack of response.

Speaking from experience, making a disconnect between what we know about God and what we've been shown about God is extremely difficult.

If this sounds like you, then it is likely you have been living with an unawareness of just how big the God-shaped hole in your heart really is. But now that you are faced with an addiction that's made you powerless, you're left only to rely on God to help you overcome it.

A God that you may not even trust or truly even know that well.

We'll work toward repairing that hole in a later chapter.

I became a Christian at sixteen years old, and that was when the severity of my addiction became impossible to ignore.

Pornography use took me places I never thought I would go. It kept me there longer than I intended to stay. And it cost me more than I wanted to pay.

Not only had pornography taken over my life in more ways than one, but pornography became an idol.

Most of us know that an idol is something that is worshiped. So you could say, I worshiped pornography each time I placed my desire for lust above God.

When we do that as Christians, we are telling God that we don't need Him. We're telling Him that we find greater pleasure in serving our sin than we do in serving our Savior.

27

Jesus says in John 8:34, "I tell you, everyone who sins is a slave to sin."

It took me a long time to see that I was worshiping a false god and to see that I wasn't in control of the pornography at all, but instead, the pornography, through sin, was controlling me all along.

I had actually become a slave to it. Pornography had become my master.

John 10:10 says, "The thief comes only to steal and kill and destroy." And this is exactly what my choice to sin with pornography did to me.

Pornography stole my innocence at a very early age.

Pornography killed my relationships by keeping me from creating any.

Pornography destroyed my life by taking away my life outside of the porn use.

Rock bottom looks different for everyone. While rock bottom began a couple of years prior when I began acting out inappropriately with adult (married) men, my real rock bottom, the rock bottom that changed the course of my life, occurred just a few weeks before my nineteenth birthday.

The pornography I was viewing was no longer satisfying.

The masturbation I was engaging in was no longer satisfying.

The cybersex chat rooms were no longer satisfying.

Performing phone sex for men was no longer satisfying.

I desired something more.

I desired something new.

But what?

The only thing left was the physical act of sex.

I was of course too hung up on how others perceived me to make an advance on anyone I knew. And I was far too insecure with my body and with men in general to ever take that leap with a stranger.

To me it was one thing to perform sexual acts with men, to men, but it was something else entirely to allow a man to actually see me naked, let alone touch me.

But the addiction kept demanding more.

When I wasn't too busy looking at porn, I remember there were always ads on the sides of web pages for anonymous sexual encounters.

It didn't take me long to find such a website and begin browsing. In just a matter of minutes, I found a suitable candidate and scheduled a hookup.

On yet another nothing-out-of-the-ordinary autumn afternoon, I waited in a cheap—and might I add freezing—hotel room for my hookup to arrive.

Even as I write this I can't believe what I was doing.

Not only was I putting myself in an incredibly dangerous situation—meeting up with a complete stranger—I was willing to have sex with this person.

Knock. Knock.

The stranger was here.

Yet, I literally could not move a muscle. Chalk it up to adrenaline.

Knock. Knock.

I stood up to answer the beckoning door, when my legs buckled beneath me, causing me to fall immediately to my knees . . .

It was in that moment, for the first time since accepting Christ almost three years earlier, that I truly heard His voice.

"I have something better for you . . . if only you'd give this to Me."

I conceded in the only way I knew how.

I closed my eyes, as tightly as I could. And waited.

The knocking finally stopped.

And I threw up right there on the floor. I composed myself and went home.

I was not satisfied, but I was ultimately relieved that I didn't do what I had set out to do. But again saw with new eyes how powerful my desire had become.

Exactly one week later, I found myself back in my old life.

The same old routine of ever so delicately balancing good and evil.

This time I was at a Christian concert that I had helped put together with some students at my church's youth group.

Feeling like a fraud, remembering where I had been just a week earlier, I wandered around until I found a place I could easily hide and get through the evening unnoticed.

That's when I saw the merchandise table for a friend's band. I had known him for a little while; he had been volunteering at the youth group for some time. I figured it would be okay for me to hang out over there and look busy.

They were already heading onstage but I noticed his wife, Anne, was sitting there. I had only met her a couple of times before then, but always thought she was nice, and I knew I could easily make small talk, if necessary.

She was a few years older than me, but we got to talking about all kinds of things, even laughing some and enjoying the concert, when all of a sudden she said to me, "I used to struggle with a pornography addiction, and it is kinda creeping up again. I need someone to help me keep that in check. Do you think you could help me with that?"

I was stunned.

Almost choking on my Diet Coke, I simply said to her, "Yeah, sure, that would be fine."

You need to understand that I had never known *anyone* who had a pornography addiction, let alone another woman.

Was she messing with me?

Did she somehow learn of my secret and was just trying to freak me out? I remained silent. Confused. Scared. Ready to run.

The musicians finished their set with one more song, called "Silence." But unlike the song title, the noise in my head was deafening. Blaring every possible scenario and every possible next step I could come up with. Working up my next lie.

It appeared I had another choice.

I could walk away from my only chance for help. Or I could jump in headfirst and accept this gift sitting across the table from me.

When the song ended, I swung my body back around to face this woman that God was to use to change my life.

I asked her again about what she had asked me before. She explained in great detail about how pornography was the thorn in her side since she was a teenager. How she actually threw her computer away in order to free her life of porn but that lately she'd felt tempted again.

She explained that there were very few resources for women porn addicts, but that there was free computer software that worked as accountability, instead of filtering. That we could install it on our respective computers and I'd receive her reports.

Interrupting her, I just came out with it: "Me too."

It was in that moment I let someone into my darkness for the first time.

I shared with her all about the last eight years of my entrapment.

How I simply couldn't stop. How I had hit rock bottom the week before. How I had no clue how to climb back out.

We agreed in that moment that we would help each other.

God used her to breathe new life back into my lungs and to shine light into a place that had never seen the light of day before. So that's my story. That's me.

Of course it isn't easy to be so raw and honest about where I have been. But when I consider the alternative. The darkness. The isolation.

I gotta tell you there's no comparison on the other side of it. So now it is your turn to make the choice.

Walk away. Or jump in.

Chapter 1

FROM WOUNDED TO HEALED

So you decided to jump in. Good for you.

Now that you've read my story, I'm going to level with you. I know that I was somewhat lucky. I know that we aren't always graced with the chance to go second.

The chance to share our struggle after someone has already shared hers.

You might be thinking, *So what about me? Where's my chance to go second?* Sometimes, maybe even most of the time, it seems we're just out here on our own to figure this out.

I get that. I really do. Which is why I designed this book to be your chance.

You see, I've just shared my story with you. And I did so first—well before I asked you to spill your guts.

It is my hope—no, it is my prayer—that you will accept my sharing first as an invitation for you to go second.

Throughout this book, we will go step-by-step to healing from pornography use. And we will do so together. With each step, I will go first by sharing with you additional pieces of my own story and then provide you the opportunities to respond. The steps are simple. And there are just five of them.

The acronym SCARS will serve as our road map. These steps are adapted from the Twelve Steps of Sexaholics Anonymous (SA). It is not my intention to reinvent the wheel or knock the great work of SA or Alcoholics Anonymous. Or to appear like I know more about addiction recovery.

That is simply untrue. In fact, the complete Twelve Steps of SA[3] are listed on page 143, and I strongly encourage you to work through them.

I know in today's age of instant gratification that we have attention spans that are next to nothing, so asking commitment to twelve of anything can be overwhelming.

And I realize how busy the life of a woman is.

Even some of the allure of pornography for women is that it is quick, easily accessible, and instantly gratifying.

On some level anyway.

However, pornography is not the problem. Masturbation is not the problem. Our compulsive sexual behaviors are not the problem.

They are merely the symptoms of something much, much

bigger. The symptoms of a core, unhealed woundedness. A wound that has been filled with a whole bunch of junk to deter from and ignore what's really going on.

When we first enter into this journey, we're so focused on being healed of our compulsive sexual behavior. Healed from the wounds those things have caused. But what really needs to happen is the healing of our core, unhealed woundedness. The unseen woundedness that led us here.

Most of us don't want to face what's unseen. But that is exactly what has to happen in order to be healed. Fully healed.

So, You're Skeptical

The use of the word "scars" to explain the steps of recovery actually came as a late-night revelation. I was reminded of Thomas in John 20. Such a doubter, he just had to see the scars on Christ's hands and on His side before he would believe it was really Jesus, raised from the dead.

I can understand his doubt. I too am a skeptic. Jesus could be standing in front of me, and I might still ask to see an ID.

I'd probably be the same way as Thomas, and I can bet you might be the same way too. Because again, you want to know that person who is standing in front of you, trying to help, can in fact understand where you've been.

Christ's scars served as a proof to Thomas that Christ was for real.

We must first expose our core woundedness for what it is. A deep pain that has simply been medicated and bandaged by our destructive behavior but was never truly cared for properly.

A wound that was dealt with (through avoidance and denial), but was not healed.

I'm not going to lie; exposing our unhealed woundedness can be downright ugly. It can be painful. It can even be infected by years of neglect.

Just as the scars on Christ's hands and side proved who He was to Thomas, the scars left behind from our own wounds prove His healing in us.

But when we finally expose it, clean out the junk that's been filling it up, and fill it again with good, healthy things, over time and with proper care, the wound will actually begin to heal.

And in its place will be only a scar. A reminiscence of what was. Not of what still is.

Scars in and of themselves aren't bad. Scars are a sign that healing from something traumatic has taken place. Scars are a reminder of where we've been. Scars show others that we know what they're going through and that we may actually be able to help. In fact, there's a saying that scars are like tattoos with better stories.

What better story could be told than one of a healed and redeemed life?

Just as the scars on Christ's hands and side proved who He was to Thomas, the scars left behind from our own wounds prove His healing in us. He is after all the only true Healer.

Without further ado, I will introduce each of the five steps, as a prelude to what you will explore more deeply in the chapters to come. So grab a journal (you'll need one as periodic reflection questions are presented), a Bible, and maybe even a piece of chocolate.

And let's begin.

S Is for Surrender

"Today is the day that I am going to stop looking at porn . . ."

"Today's the day that I am going to live a pure life . . ."

Sound familiar? Of course it does.

All of us, at one time or another, have made these idle promises to ourselves. To God.

But what happens is a couple of days of good intentions, maybe even a couple of weeks with success in our attempts to not act out, but ultimately we stumble again. And instead of beginning, we become discouraged and fall back on what's familiar and comfortable.

Falling even harder into a routine of destruction.

Well, why does this happen to us?

Behavior modification doesn't work without first surrendering control of our behavior (emotional disorders, physical desires, mental afflictions) to God.

Surrender begins by asking the question, "Do I trust God enough to get well?"

C Is for Confession

The word *confess* means "to acknowledge." Confession of sin is an acknowledgment of sin, with the intent of seeking forgiveness. We have a scriptural promise in 1 John 1:9 that "if we confess our sins, he is faithful and just and will forgive us our sins."

Confession should not be done out of arrogance. Confession should not come from a desire to manipulate someone or a situation. Confession should not be hasty or rushed to simply get it over with. Confession should not be done out of fear.

And getting caught does not count as a confession.

Light eliminates the darkness. Shining light on your addiction will bring light to a situation that has been dark for too long.

Confession may be the scariest of the steps because it means finally opening up to another human being about what we've experienced.

But confession is nothing if not simply obedience as found in James 5:16: "Confess your sins to each other and pray for each other so that you may be healed."

If you are faithful in obedience, God will be faithful in seeing you through it.

A Is for Accountability

Most of us know that accountability is about being responsible, or answerable, for our behavior and actions. However, addicts are resistant to accountability more often than not because of the notion that they will be told what to do and how to do it.

Even reading this idea of accountability may be rubbing some of you the wrong way. But it goes deeper than just dos and don'ts.

For as long as we've been addicted, our basic MO has been to lie or deceive others in order to keep our addictive behaviors a secret. We've told so many lies that we may not even trust ourselves anymore.

Or know where one lie ends and another lie begins.

The act of accountability restores the character that has been lost in us and makes us into women of integrity.

Integrity. Something most of us have been living without for too long.

This is done by not simply being held accountable to our actions but being held accountable to growing spiritually, growing closer and more intimate with God.

But accountability cannot be done alone. Recovery cannot be done alone. Proverbs 12:15 (NLT) says, "Fools think their own way is right, but the wise listen to others."

So it is vitally important first, to surround yourself with other believers. People who are going to lift you up—not pull you down or be an enabler of your past decisions. Find a healthy church, and a small group or Bible study where you can grow in community with other women.

Second, pinpoint someone who can act as your mentor, guide, or trusted friend.

This person should be female and preferably someone who has walked the same road you're on right now with a track record of at least a year of freedom.

If you can't find someone who meets those criteria, then find a pastor, biblical counselor, or someone else of spiritual authority to adopt this role.

Find someone who will hold you accountable and form a plan for when you are tempted (which no doubt is going to happen). A mentor provides encouragement, an ear to listen, prayerful support, and will be a model and guide for you on how to live a life without porn.

And third, join a support group.

On pages 145–149 of this book, you'll find resources for locating groups meeting online and locally around the country.

A support group will allow you to commune with women who know exactly where you are because they are exactly where you are. And you can help one another through the recovery process.

I believe fully in the power of community through the body of Christ to help break the cycle of addiction. Of any addiction. I so wish there had been a women's group when I began my journey to freedom.

R Is for Responsibility

By accepting responsibility, we begin looking less inside ourselves and more to the outside—where our actions may have had an impact on others.

You may even need to create a personal inventory of how your addiction has harmed others: whether the harm was physical, emotional, spiritual, or even financial.

This isn't about filling you with shame or regret. Not at all.

Remember what John wrote in 1 John 1:9, "If we confess our sins, he is faithful and just and will forgive us our sins."

Our sin is covered. We shall feel no more shame.

Be gentle with yourself as you create this inventory. Talk it through with your mentor or support group.

This step is about growing in maturity. Moving away from denial, blame, or self-pity to accepting responsibility for your own actions.

Refer to the story of the prodigal son in Luke 15.

This is a beautiful account of someone taking full responsibility for their behavior and acknowledging that their behavior didn't affect just themselves personally, but the effect it may have had on those in their lives and on the heart of God.

The Last S Stands for Sharing

This is the final step in the SCARS sequence and should be done after *at least* six weeks of freedom. It may need to be longer for you.

It is my firm belief that God never wastes an experience.

And sharing is about knowing that you have a story, and that sharing that story is an essential part of your healing.

You will need to share again and again, because we can never finish rejoicing in the work the Lord has done in us. There's always someone else to tell.

First, prepare your story by writing it out. Once you have written your story, you'll begin to consider who may need to hear it. Practice telling your story to these people, and then pray about how God may want to use your story further.

If you had told me fifteen, ten, or even five years ago that I would be writing a book that exposes my whole story and be the founding director of an anti-pornography ministry, I would have laughed in your face.

But that is how big the God we serve is.

He can take what was once a broken vessel and piece it together again. He intends to use your story in remarkable ways. And His refinement is most often the best part.

Testimonial:
AmyChristine Comes Clean

Pornography has turned my life upside down. My first exposure to pornography was through a childhood friend at the age of eight, but the curiosity exploded when the Internet made its debut.

Like all young people, I developed a normal desire to know more about sex. My parents and church taught me nothing; the only knowledge I had was from health class at school, so I turned to the Internet to find out more. What I didn't realize was that those beginning moments of searching the World Wide Web for information on sex soon snared me in its web.

I was hooked—I became engrossed in searching the Internet for entertainment any chance I could get. In my teens, it started with chat rooms but also led to searching for erotic stories. In my twenties, the search exploded as I became desperate for more. I began actively searching for pornography to fill my growing needs. What started with pictures soon led to videos, all being readily available on my parents' unfiltered computer. Then, as if dealing with pornography wasn't enough, I was now adding masturbation to this ongoing struggle.

Words cannot begin to convey the amount of shame I have endured while living with these sexual sins. Chains began having their grip on me at the tender age of eight years old. But despite this shame (or because of it), I became a follower of Jesus Christ when I was fifteen. Now, as a thirty-year-old Christian woman, I am still fighting these chains, and let me assure you, it is not easy being a Christian woman struggling with this highly taboo sin of pornography.

I did not date much in my teens or twenties. I didn't need to, since in my world, pornography was my relationship. I didn't need anything from anyone. Pornography was a constant friend, which now I label as false intimacy.

Pornography is a drug of the mind. I could use it, and no one needed to know. Unlike if I had used street drugs, however, I never had to interact with anyone, so, on the surface, I could maintain the "goodie-goodie" label. As time elapsed, pornography became a daily routine, but there were often days where I had to search out deeper and darker things to get the same result.

In late 2009, I reached the end of my rope. Living with this oppressive shame and guilt, in combination with my profession as a flight attendant, severely affected my health. Because I'd spend hours a night searching out pornography, I was sleep deprived in a job that already had its own challenges of sleep deprivation. My spiritual sickness was now leading to physical sickness, but I still couldn't seem to stop. In early 2010, I was desperate to make a change. In February 2010, I turned thirty, and I didn't want to go one more decade addicted to pornography.

The biggest jump start has been accountability. I have a wonderful spiritual mom who mentors me and has held me accountable. I placed filters on my computer and even went to the radical extreme of giving up my laptop for nine months, since I had to remove all access. Computers that are not filtered or protected are dangerous to the pornography addict, much like giving an alcoholic a beer to hold and expecting him not to drink.

And while accountability is a great step in the right direction, I also need fellowship. For me, fellowship in a church body is critical, yet my job as a flight attendant often causes me to work weekends, thus curtailing the very fellowship I need and crave. There has also been the need to belong, and thankfully, this past spring the Lord led me to Dirty Girls Ministries, where I found other women (both believers and nonbelievers) who struggle as I have. Many stories are similar to mine. I have continued my journey by joining a recovery group and combined that with Christian counseling.

Sadly, porn has consumed twenty-two years of my life. I lost part of my childhood, my innocence, as well as time, energy, relationships, potential relationships, my walk with God, and now my health. I know that freedom is possible because I've seen and heard the testimonies of others. That's why I know that this journey is not meant to be walked alone.

Truthfully, I feel like I am moving at a snail's pace. I know God's desire for me is to be whole, and I will not give up no matter how slow the process seems. And while I have my days of feeling this journey will never end, I've also tasted freedom too. The enemy of our souls wants us in isolation and in the pit, but with Christ's strength and grace, I will not remain in that pit anymore.

Chapter 2

YOU ARE HERE

If you've ever shopped in a mall, then you've likely used one of those handy store locator maps. You know, one of those large lighted boards that displays where every single store is located on the premises.

From high-end stores that hold all of the shoes and purses we can't afford to the Orange Julius stand ready to quench the thirst caused by the abdominal workout of trying on jeans, the store locator map helps us to see where we are so we can find where it is we want to go to next.

The first thing you look for is that little androgynous figure that reads, "You Are Here." We do this because we can't find where we want to go until we first know where we are.

The following exercise will serve as your map. Yes, *your* map.

As you personalize it with your answers, it will become more and more yours. No one's map is the same. Your addiction is full of personal detours, derailments, and wrong turns.

This map will help you to personally navigate through where you've been, to see where you are now, in order to make getting to where you want to go a whole lot easier.

I know these things are difficult to face, and if you are in it, it just seems easier to turn back around and leave.

I also know that the idea of going back and digging up the past is an overwhelming thought and could be building up anxiety in you right now.

Rest assured that God is much more concerned about where you are headed than where you have been. We serve a God of second chances.

Take Your Pulse

Before we can break free from pornography, we need to admit our true condition and know exactly what we are dealing with. That is where the Personal Inventory comes in.

There are many sexual addiction inventory tests out there, but what makes this one a bit different is that it targets just pornography and pornography-related behavior. And provides space to reflect on how these personally relate to you.

This is not an "Am I an addict?" test. You wouldn't be reading this book if you didn't already believe pornography use has become a problem for you.

While there is nothing scientific about the following questions, they will help you put pen to paper so you can see how severe the situation is and how much control pornography has over YOUR life. It is then and only then that YOU can begin to take the proper steps toward freedom.

No formula. Just the bare-bones facts.

Rest assured that God is much more concerned about where you are headed than where you have been. We serve a God of second chances.

This inventory is only the beginning of a long process, but you don't have to do it alone. If at any time during this inventory or throughout this book you need the support of an understanding community, visit http://dirtygirlsministries.com to connect with me, my team, and hundreds of other women just like you on this journey.

As you work your way through the inventory, keep in mind these four essential elements of pornography-addiction recovery and how honestly completing this inventory helps:

First, understanding the seriousness of sexual sin.

Second, evaluating where you are vulnerable to sexual sin.

Third, confessing honestly where you have messed up.

And last, committing to sexual purity from this day forward.

"Walk in a manner worthy of the Lord, fully pleasing to him, bearing fruit in every good work and increasing in the knowledge of God. May you be strengthened with all power, according to his glorious might"(Colossians 1:10–11 ESV).

So, where are you? Let's find out together.

Choose the inventory that best describes your present relationship with pornography and pornography related behavior.

- The Personal Inventory for those still in bondage (see page 127) is for those who believe themselves to be presently addicted to pornography and/or pornography related sexual behavior.
- The Personal Inventory for those free from bondage (see page 135) is for those who have had an on again/off again relationship with pornography and pornography-related behavior, but have abstained for at least six months. It is important to remember that just because you are no longer acting out, it doesn't mean your wounds are healed.

Go Ahead, Just Do It

Turn to the back of the book and take one of the inventories.

⎯⎯⎯⎯⎯⎯⎯⎯⎯⎯⎯⎯⎯⎯⎯⎯⎯→

There, that wasn't so bad. Right?

If you are working through this book as a part of a group, share what you learned from this inventory at your next meeting. If you are working through this book on your own, share with a trusted friend, church leader, or counselor.

However, please don't get caught up in past behavior or feel shameful about the actions you took. What you have done comes

As you move forward and continue to make an account for your past and present behaviors, it is important that you begin to make it a priority to live a whole, healthy life.

as no shock to God. And frankly, if I were sitting right there with you (and I hope you feel like I am) none of this comes as a shock to me either.

How could it? If everything we do was about the behavior, about the actions, it would be a lot easier to not do wrong. We would all be perfect all the time. Behavior is just a piece of the whole self.

Following Jesus is not just about behavioral modification. We've established that behavior modification begins with surrendering our whole selves to God's control.

It's about transformation of the heart. It's not just about your actions; it's about your heart and your motives for why you do the things you do.

As you move forward and continue to make an account for your past and present behaviors, it is important that you begin to make it a priority to live a whole, healthy life.

We tend to appease one area of ourselves: behavior. But in fact when even just one area suffers, the whole person suffers.

A whole healthy person has five basic needs. And wouldn't you know it? I have a bit of a road map for that too. These have been adapted from *L.I.F.E. Guide for Women*[4] by Marnie C. Ferree.

These are the basic, but absolutely necessary, needs for wholeness:

- Physical (eating well, exercise)
- Behavioral (sobriety, attending a support group, engaging in hobbies)
- Relational (connecting with safe friends)
- Personal (receiving counseling, awareness of feeling)
- Spiritual (corporate worship, personal time in prayer)

This leads us to the first section for reflection. The space provided will not always be adequate, so please use a journal to complete the exercises in each reflection area. It may be a good idea to keep your journal with you for easy access and space to write.

Becoming clean

1. By now you should have taken your Personal Inventory Test. The next step is to create a time line for your addiction. List your sexual acting out (including relationships) in a time line fashion beginning with your first exposure to sexuality. Include your present and your past efforts to get help. I know it may be emotionally challenging and may be overwhelming to dig through your past. So take your time. But it is crucial to know where you've been, before you can move on to where you want to go.

2. Now that you know where you've been, where is it you want to go? Write it down and keep this goal someplace you will able to see it often.

3. How does it make you feel when you think of what it would be like to be free from your pornography addiction?

4. As the saying goes, "If you keep doing what you've always done, you'll keep getting what you've always gotten." Describe how this statement has been true in your own life.

5. Over the next six weeks, evaluate yourself daily in the five needs of healthy living. List out each of the five needs (physical, behavioral, relational, personal, and spiritual) and what you are doing each day to fulfill them. You may begin to notice imbalances in a couple of areas. If you do, take that opportunity to work on those areas in the days to follow.

Testimonial:
Sarah Comes Clean

Six years ago my life ended. Or rather, began.

Early in January of that year I confessed to an affair, both emotional and physical, that I'd been engaging in for a few years. It was the end of an old way of life for me (and for my husband) and the beginning of something amazing and grace-filled.

Caustic communication with sarcasm as its core value, excessive drinking, and elaborate money-spending habits were just some of the bad practices we'd built as a couple. Add to that regular viewing of pornography and no boundaries in what we watched or how we each interacted with the opposite sex, and we had a marriage ripe for disaster.

My husband had been expelled from his Christian middle school for selling porn videos out of his locker. That's right. There's no need to explain in detail, but he, like many men, had struggled with pornography from the time he was very young.

During the first few years of our marriage, both Internet and video pornography became a regular part of our bedroom activities. Even though he introduced me to it, I was a willing participant in the viewing and allowed the images and desires to invade me until mine became almost as great an addiction as my husband was dealing with.

He looked at videos. I looked at erotica websites. And then together we used pornography as a "third party" when we were with each other.

The cycle that pornography created was destructive. It zapped my husband's desire for me, but it fed my craving for frequent sex. As a result, we became so unevenly matched in desire that most evenings one or both of us was so frustrated with the other that it became a constant source of battle.

Pornography did not *cause* me to have an affair. But it fed my desires in unhealthy ways and was a factor in my downward spiral. It became something I relied on for arousal. It became something I depended on during our times of sexual interaction. And then it became something I engaged in alone when he was gone on business trips or working late.

Finally, our lives came to a standstill. I had confessed to an affair with a friend of my husband, God had broken my heart, and I was ready to do anything and everything to fix the mess that I'd made. Although my husband hadn't engaged in an extramarital affair, he was as much in need of redemption as I was.

During one of the first sessions with our marriage counselor, she said something like, "An affair is not a reason for marital problems; it's a symptom."

Right. So all of the other things we were engaging in both individually and as a couple were feeding our selfish habits, one of which was a horribly self-destructive affair that I'd been fostering. We, in essence, had a sick marriage, and one of the results of that sick marriage was my affair.

We spent a couple of years living like "monks," getting rid of movies and DVDs and cutting the cable to our TV—anything that would be detrimental to our crawl back to Christ. We poured out alcohol, read the Bible from cover to cover, and spent hours and hours in counseling sessions.

God had so breathtakingly changed us in January of that year that halting the pornography was just a given at that point. We were so ready to have our lives completely turned around by God that locking down our computers was a no-brainer. Our hearts were different: new and alive. The thought of pornography was distasteful to me by then, and I didn't want to do anything to jeopardize my "newlywed" relationship with my husband or my "newlywed" relationship with God. I disciplined myself to try to forget the pictures that had been burned into my mind from years of viewing destructive pornographic images.

Most of it is habit by now. As a couple, we know that when a television show or movie goes south, we need to switch the channel or turn it off altogether. We still don't have a cable connection to our home, and we've tightly locked down our home computers.

I've been able to live six years pornography-free, both in my mind and in practice. I owe it to a heart changed and softened by Christ and to boundaries that we've put in place and adhered to as a couple.

And I'll never go back.

Chapter 3

S-SURRENDER:

Trusting the Healer

When I was fourteen, a new church was about to open just a few blocks from my house. One of my mom's coworkers (in fact, I think it was her supervisor) invited us to a fall festival they were putting on in celebration of their new building's grand opening. Of course she dragged me to it, thinking that I'd have a great time.

It turned out the festival wasn't the only part of my mom's clever plan. She was also planning to go to their opening service that coming Sunday.

It had been a long time since we had been to church. My recollection of church before then was when I was just eight years old. Well before my pornography-viewing days. We had just transitioned from Catholic church to Baptist church. My dad had stopped attending Mass, and my mom wanted return to her Protestant roots.

One morning in Sunday school when the gospel was shared, I raised my hand to show I wanted to accept Jesus as my Lord and Savior. When I look back now, I realize I raised my hand only because some other kids did. I was new to this church, and I didn't want to appear like I didn't know what was going on.

Again, it was all about perception with me.

Soon after my so-called decision, a man came to our home to speak with me more about what it meant to follow Jesus. But all I can remember about our talk was a story he shared about accidently cutting his nose while shaving that morning.

Perhaps he was self-conscious about the cut showing.

All that to say I wasn't that excited about going to another new church or being around other church-type people. Or pretending I had it all together.

But to my surprise, this church was different.

No nuns. No old dude in a white collar passing out cardboard bread. No choirs. No pews. No man talking about cutting his nose shaving.

It was actually pretty great.

The "guy speaking" was easy to understand, and the "guy singing" just happened to be incredibly attractive (hope he's not reading this!). It was the notion of seeing him again and my mom's nagging that brought me back the next Sunday. And the next. And then the next.

After several months of just going through the motions of sitting in a cushy seat on Sunday morning, my mom began to talk to me about something called "youth group." The very idea of being around a group of "kumbaya" teenagers was out of the question. After all, I had no friends to speak of, and I didn't need any.

Especially not good God-fearing ones who would be able to smell the disgrace of my pornography use all over me.

That all changed one afternoon when a senior in my high school invited me, a mere freshman, to go watch him play in a band.

It doesn't take a genius to figure out the equation that if a senior guy invites a freshman girl to do anything, she's gonna do it.

Particularly a freshman girl as insecure as I was.

Unfortunately, he meant at youth group. The same youth group my mom was trying to get me to go to. Apparently he had seen me attending church services regularly on Sunday morning, but knew I hadn't made my way to youth group yet. Sneaky senior.

By the time summer came, I was nearly sixteen years old and by some miracle my secret life with porn remained undiscovered, even though I'd then been involved in church for almost two years. And I was actually beginning to enjoy going.

But then one day my mom as well as "very tall youth group speaker guy" told me about something called Super Summer.

Apparently Super Summer was some sort of camp for kumbaya teenagers to swim with T-shirts over their suits while singing about Jesus. I had no interest in going, but knew it would make my mom happy and perhaps even mean some alone time with aforementioned senior.

But it also meant five days away from home.

Five days without access to pornography. Five days without being able to masturbate. Five days without the only things that made me feel alive . . . that made me feel anything at all.

It was then that for the first time I began to see the extent of how my behavior was affecting my life.

Not understanding why I was

I thought it was going to be the most miserable five days of my life, but a funny thing begins to happen when focus changes from satisfying self to satisfying Jesus.

so resistant to the idea of going to camp, my mom began to push the issue. I played it off that I was scared of leaving home for so many nights. Up until then I had never left home before, so it was easy for her to believe that.

But when "very tall youth group speaker guy," also known as Grant, pushed me to go, I began to feel the pressure building and was becoming harder to lie about why I didn't want to go.

In order to keep good face and not bring about any unnecessary speculation, I knew I had to go. So I hopped a bus and made my way to camp.

I thought it was going to be the most miserable five days of my life, but a funny thing begins to happen when focus changes from satisfying self to satisfying Jesus.

It only took a few hours into the camp experience for me to almost forget about the fact that I couldn't look at porn.

I surrendered fully to the camp experience. When I did so, I could see and hear things more clearly than I had in a very long time. Including just how miserable I really was. I began to feel the mask start to come off.

When the pornography is shut off and you're left with only God, do you trust that He will be enough to sustain you?

One evening the "camp speaker guy," Andy, presented a talk about accepting Jesus as Lord and Savior. Similar to the one I had heard when I was eight years old in Sunday school. But now it was as if I was hearing it for the first time.

When he spoke the words, "You have a Father in heaven who loves you unconditionally," it was as if the world around me froze.

A Father in heaven loves me unconditionally? Like, all of me? Even the ugly, shameful parts that I never let anyone else see?

It was in that moment, I was adopted into the arms of Jesus. I had accepted Jesus as my Lord and Savior and it was real this time.

However, it would be a couple of years before I'd surrender my behavior fully.

Most women who struggle with pornography addiction more often than not feel alone. We've isolated ourselves for so long that not only have we isolated ourselves from those closest to us, but also we isolate ourselves from God. And before long we don't trust anyone anymore. Paranoia sets in.

The feeling of everyone around us knowing our affliction and already judging us beyond repair.

We buy the lie of the enemy that the shame of our actions is too great for anyone, including God, to understand. The problem isn't unbelief that we're capable of overcoming our sin and afflictions. It may feel at times that it is impossible, but we all know deep down that if we could face God and be surrendered to the process, we could indeed overcome it.

The problem is lack of trust.

When the pornography is shut off and you're left with only God, do you trust that He will be enough to sustain you?

If your answer to that question is no, don't feel shame.

Asking the Right Question

This is all a part of the recovery process and is even mentioned at the healing pool in John 5:1–6.

Some time later, Jesus went up to Jerusalem for a feast of the Jews. Now there is in Jerusalem near the Sheep Gate a pool, which in Aramaic is called Bethesda and which is surrounded by five covered colonnades. Here a great number of disabled people used to lie—the blind, the lame, the paralyzed. One who was there had been an invalid for thirty-eight years. When Jesus saw him lying there and learned that he had been in this condition for a long time, he asked him, "Do you want to get well?"

"Do you want to get well?" What kind of question was that? Why would a man, who was sick and crippled for thirty-eight years, not want to get well? It is easy.

We are often the most comfortable in our own paralysis.

Yet, I'd venture to say that most of us are extremely uncomfortable with our sin.

No, our addiction to pornography is not something we're so comfortable with that we brag about it to our friends and wear a homemade puff paint T-shirt for all to see.

If that were true, we would never walk in shame.

We are actually extremely uncomfortable with it. But it is what we cling to because it is what we know. It is familiar to us.

There's a huge difference between being comfortable and just having a feeling of familiarity. Complacency.

The man at the healing pool wasn't comfortable with being an invalid, but he had grown complacent and familiar with his state.

By asking, "Do you want to get well?" Jesus isn't just playing a game of Captain Obvious.

He is asking the man to examine his heart.

Your addiction is nothing if not first a heart issue.

In the following chapters, we will look in greater detail at what it will mean to fully surrender your addiction to God. But in this chapter we will examine what makes us reluctant even to begin the healing process.

For thirty-eight years the man at the healing pool came up with excuses for why he couldn't reach the healing pool.

"I have no one to help me into the pool when the water is stirred. While I am trying to get in, someone else goes down ahead of me" (v. 7).

The dude wants to get well, but repeatedly gives excuses for why being free isn't possible. He is saying these things to Jesus. Seems dumb.

And yet we do the same thing. Even when we have the opportunity for healing, we choose double-mindedness. Sure, a part of us would like to be freed from the sin. Sure, a part of us would like to live a life of purity. Sure, a part of us would like to walk with our chins up and shame free.

But do we really want to get well? Or should the question really be: Are we willing to do whatever it takes to be healed?

Does that question make you uncomfortable? It should.

If you're already going through the inventory in your mind of what you will need to give up in order to really get well . . . Good.

For many of us, our addiction has become our closest friend. The only viable thing we have to cling to when the day is done. It is hard to even think about life without it.

Going back to John 5, the part we don't see is how this man went from being an invalid who for thirty-eight years couldn't even muster up enough will to scoot himself to the healing pool, to all of sudden trying to stand on his feet.

Can you imagine what that must have felt like for him?

Was he scared? Was he excited? Was he possibly a little angry?

Standing up was likely something this man hadn't attempted to do in many, many years. Maybe even since the day he became paralyzed. His legs were probably too weak to even support his body weight.

And yet he stood up.

He didn't have trouble believing that Jesus could heal him. But it was through faith alone that he rose to his feet and was sick no more.

He trusted Jesus enough to stand up.

This Brings Us to the Heart of the Whole Issue

Most people who struggle with pornography addiction don't trust anyone, out of shame and control. This distrust of people causes us to isolate ourselves, and yet we are surprised when we find ourselves so alone.

Not only do we isolate ourselves from those around us, we isolate ourselves from God. Shame, control, and distrust once again keep us from seeking help.

The problem isn't unbelief that you can overcome your addiction.

But when the porn is removed and you're face-to-face with God, do you trust that He will be enough to sustain you?

If your answer to that question is no, don't feel shame.

This is all a part of the healing process.

In Mark 9 (see verses 17–29), a father brings his demon-possessed son to Jesus' disciples in order to be healed, but the disciples were unsuccessful in driving the spirit out of him.

In order to heal we must first restore our view of God, and believe He is able to do all things.

So the boy's father pleads with Jesus to help.

Jesus asks him, "How long has he been like this?"

The boy's father answers, "From childhood . . . if you can do anything, take pity on us and help us."

Jesus then answers, "'If you can'? Everything is possible for him who believes."

Immediately the boy's father exclaims, "I do believe; help me overcome my unbelief!"

Jesus then commands the spirit out the boy, and he was healed.

In private the disciples asked Jesus why they were unable to drive it out themselves.

Jesus replied, "This kind can come out only by prayer."

In order to heal, we must first restore our view of God and believe He is able to do all things.

Healing can't be left just to ourselves.

Becoming clean

1. In the past, what has kept you from embracing the process of

2. Why are you embracing the process now?

3. Have you ever made up excuses about how hard it is to find help? If so, what excuses did you make?

4. Write a description of your present view of God. What is God like in your mind?

5. God is: everlasting, faithful, good, generous, holy, unchangeable, infinite, just, loving, merciful, all-powerful, all-present, all-knowing, sovereign, and wise.[5]

   - From this list, choose five that you find easy to believe about God. Write them down, and journal how it is you believe these attributes to be true.
   - Now choose five attributes of God that you have difficultly believing. Write them down, and journal why it is you struggle with these attributes. Pray this week for God to help you overcome your unbelief, and journal your responses.

Testimonial:
Chelsea Comes Clean

At eleven years old, I stumbled across someone's sexual fantasy they had written and posted on the Internet. I was intrigued and reread the story several times before moving on. Eventually, I figured out this kind of literature was called erotica and started searching online for it.

One time I showed my younger sister what I was reading, thinking she'd enjoy it too. After seeing her disgusted reaction, I decided not to tell anyone else. I didn't want to give up the high I got from reading those stories and became skilled at ignoring the little voice in my head saying, *This isn't good!*

It didn't take me long to start masturbating to the things I read. As I slid deeper into it, I did it more frequently. At one point, I was reading several stories daily for months. Every once in a while, I would hear things at youth group and church about pornography and feel convicted.

I would try to reduce my habit to a few times a week or stop looking for a few months altogether, but always went back eventually.

Being raised in a Christian home, I had plenty of access to books like *Every Man's Battle* and *Not Even a Hint*. I read those books cover to cover, hoping to find something that would break my addiction, but remained just as alone and discouraged as ever.

I knew there had to be other women out there in this same situation, but no one was talking about it. I considered starting a support group for women with sexual addictions, but was afraid no one would show up.

In 2007, I went into a yearlong internship program at my church. I shared a bedroom with three other girls, and our only bathroom with five other girls. Realizing I was the only one with any sexual addiction of any kind was very discouraging. I got dirty looks and attitude from my accountability partner, who walked in on me sinning several times. My mentor couldn't understand why it was so difficult for me to stop.

I even put up Scripture on my ceiling so I'd see it while lying in bed, but realized I could avoid looking at the ceiling while sinning to avoid guilt.

One day, a friend told me she thought if I really wanted to stop, I would stop. Offended, I told her she had no idea what she was talking about.

Later, as I processed that conversation, I realized she was right. Logically, this was something I already knew, but that day it really hit me in a deep way that I actually had a choice in this matter.

During my internship, we were required to spend at least ten hours in God's presence, i.e., in the prayer room, soaking in His presence, learning how to meditate on the Word. We were also required to memorize Scripture. This did a great deal for my healing. I resisted temptation for the rest of the internship.

As the internship came to a close in 2008, a theme started to appear in my walk: He made it very clear to me that I was in a season of preparation, and needed to use this time wisely because some big changes were coming my way soon. He kept reminding me how valuable I was, and how many amazing things He had in store for me. This season lasted four months, when I spent a great deal of time just letting Him love and heal me. I learned how to be purposeful with how I spent my time. I spent a lot of time being mentored by an older woman and observing how she lived her life. At the end of this season, I met my husband.

Since I married my husband in 2009, we have learned to stay on guard together, as this area of pornography is a weakness for him too. We have a battle plan that we adjust as needed. We each have one friend of our same sex that we are accountable to on a weekly basis, and we also remain brutally honest with each other.

I am tempted to read erotica much less frequently now than before I got married, because now my sexual needs are being met; but keeping my thought life pure remains a daily decision.

Don't get me wrong. Temptation didn't disappear just because I got married, but at the same time, my marriage has helped tremendously because of the level of accountability I get from my husband. He is my best friend. I try to tell my husband every single time I am tempted. I've even awakened him in the middle of the night, asking him to pray with me. He does the same when he is tempted. We pray together and fall back to sleep. Having my husband fight this alongside me has been a huge blessing and encouragement.

Gratification in sin only lasts a few moments, if even that long at all, before guilt sets in. In contrast, the joy in my marriage bed goes much deeper and lasts much longer. It is holy.

One of the most effective lies Satan used to seduce me after marriage is that I can have something better than my marriage bed. But every time I go back to erotica, I am always disappointed afterward.

Each time I resist temptation, the power this addiction has over me seems to become weaker. It is something I have to take one day at a time. Each day I decide whether I will honor Him with my thought life, with what I read, and with what I do, no matter what time of day it is, no matter how I'm feeling. I have my bad days, but those bad days continue to become farther and farther apart the more I reject those tempting thoughts.

Chapter 4

C-CONFESSION:

Out of the Darkness

I thought I was real slick.

Like Superwoman, I had two identities.

The one everyone saw, Good-Christian Crystal by day, and the one no one saw, Porn-Addicted, Hopeless Crystal by night.

Not long ago I found a school paper I wrote about my goals back when I was sixteen years old. Behind pretty words about my newfound faith and elaborate life goals hid a girl who was hopeless.

A girl entangled by pornography and sexual addiction.

I clearly remember when I wrote this paper. It was the beginning of my sophomore year of high school. My teacher at the time asked us to write a paper on what we hoped to accomplish during the remainder of our high school careers and what we hoped to do after graduation . . . and beyond.

I had just come off the high of getting saved at church camp. I was ready for things to be different. Or at least be perceived as different. No more being the quiet girl, afraid that everyone would know about my dirty little secret.

I was ready to drop the old mask and wear the new of one of a good Christian girl.

I had everyone fooled. I began to even have myself fooled.

This new mask was all about how I could show I had a relationship with God. When in reality, the only relationships I had were with pornography.

But if I were to begin the new school year off playing the part of "good Christian girl," surely no one would suspect me of having any secrets.

Certainly not those dirty ones.

I began to develop some friendships. I began singing in the honors ensemble and in the youth group band. I began leading the Christian club and participating in school events.

I had everyone fooled.

In the paper I wrote about how I wanted to save the school. Then go into the community and save everyone else. Show everyone how great God's love is and tour the country as a worship leader and have a big Christian family when I grew up.

And . . . and . . . and . . .

I began to even have myself fooled.

But I didn't have God fooled. He knew every bit of who I was pretending to be and who I really was.

I did accept Christ at summer camp, and I believed that some variant of that decision was real. But He knew that I didn't believe He loved me as much as and as unconditionally as everyone said He did.

And even while I had heard at youth group and church that His grace was "sufficient for" me, I didn't believe He could really see beyond my sin.

So it was easy to just play the part.

It became easier and easier just to be the good Christian girl in public, while confessing my indiscretions to God and to God alone in private. Thinking that since I was confessing to Him each time I messed up, that was enough.

As if that is what it means to be a Christian and to live life abundantly.

I was living life alone.

Sure, I was starting to have friends, but still hadn't really let anyone in. And no matter how good it all sounded, the idea of confessing my sins to one another, I was just too scared of what would happen if I actually did.

Would I get sent away to some clinic?

Would I lose all my new friends? Would I really have to stop looking at porn?

Pornography, masturbation, and overall compulsive sexual acting out does not just destroy our hearts, but it completely destroys our minds.

The human brain is an amazing thing. It absorbs absolutely everything.

As a pornography addict, you likely know that quite well. Another reason this addiction is so difficult to shake is because the images we've seen are somehow engraved in our minds. So even when we're not in front of the computer screen or flipping through a magazine, the scenarios continue to play out in our mind.

Even something as simple as a clothing ad can trigger our memories.

And because our brains are so powerful, the enemy uses our mind as a breeding ground to develop doubt, shame, and fear.

Remember Thomas?

Our mind is our own worst enemy when it comes to believing and acting on truth. And it is our worst enemy when it comes to confession.

Trampling on Snakes

Because the real enemy, the adversary, desires for you to not only be held in the bondage of an addiction, but further be captive by your very own mind. Through the lies he tells you and the fear caused by the "what ifs" of finally coming clean, our mind is his doorway to our heart.

God knows that on this earth we are going to have trials and troubles.

So the first step of confession has to be through the renewing of your mind as in Romans 12:2: "Do not conform any longer to the pattern of this world, but be transformed by the renewing of your mind. Then you will be able to test and approve what God's will is—his good, pleasing and perfect will."

You renew your mind and attack these debilitating lies with the weapon of truth.

Truth of the Word of God.

For example, if you're continuing to believe the lie—"The enemy's hold on my mind is too strong to break this cycle of addiction," we have the power and authority to use God's Word as a weapon for truth.

"I have given you authority to trample on snakes and scorpions and to overcome all the power of the enemy; nothing will harm you" (Luke 10:19).

The more we fill our mind with the truth of God's Word, the

less room the lies have in there to make any sort of impact on our emotions and thus, on our actions.

Confession is about going beyond simply confessing to God and taking the bold step in bringing someone else into our junk.

We were created for community. We need each other.

God knows that on this earth we are going to have trials and troubles. In fact, He never promises us an easy go at life. But even in His Word He promises a way out from temptation and demands confession from us when temptation becomes action.

James 5:16 encourages us to "confess your sins to each other and pray for each other so that you may be healed."

But why is it that confessing to others seems so much harder than confessing to God? Perhaps even confessing to God feels pretend sometimes. Almost as if confessing to God isn't real.

Confessing to God and not to others is also a form of deception. Because not only are you not being honest with those around you, but also you're likely creating lies to cover up your tracks.

When we confess to God and not also to others, we cheapen God's grace. Your sins are of no surprise to God. You won't find a person on earth who isn't carrying some piece of luggage they are ashamed about.

When God talks about healing through confession, He is talking about healing from having to be our own savior.

That is why Christ died.

It is okay to be a screwup because there's grace enough to

cover it. So we don't have to live in shame. The body of Christ, our brothers and sisters in Christ, are to be His hands and feet on earth. And His arms and ears.

Yes, confession is hard. Perhaps one of the hardest things we as Christians are called to do. But would it be hard if it weren't vitally important to our spiritual development?

I believe the harder something is, the greater God rewards the obedience.

Becoming clean

1. What lie are you buying in to when it comes to confessing your addiction to a friend, counselor, or trusted mentor?

- Write down each lie. Next to each lie, write a truth from God's Word that counteracts the lie. If you don't know any by memory, go to BibleGateway.com to search Scriptures based on keywords.

- Now, based on the Scripture you found, rewrite the lie into a truth you can recite to yourself when the enemy chimes in again.

2. Why is confession to someone face-to-face so crucial to our freedom from addiction?

3. Isaiah 61:7 says, "Instead of their shame my people will receive a double portion, and instead of disgrace they will rejoice in their inheritance; and so they will inherit a double portion in their land, and everlasting joy will be theirs." Does this passage relate to our obedience in confession? If so, how?

4. Who is someone in your life right now you could share your struggle with? Pray this week that God would not only grant you the courage to tell that person, but that He'd also provide the opportune time to share with her.

5. After you have made your confession, journal your experience describing how you did it and the person's reaction to your news.

Testimonial:
Jenny Comes Clean

I grew up in an ultraconservative family and church background, the type of environment where you don't talk about things like sex or anything related to it. My mom, in her best efforts to teach me the facts about life, provided me with a book that left me with a lot of questions that I just didn't feel comfortable asking her. At the age of seventeen, I graduated from high school a year early and set off to a secular college as a very sheltered girl, curious about sex.

Once in college, I spent a lot of time in the empty library computer room chatting online with guys in chat rooms. Because I was insecure and I was so intrigued about sex, it wasn't long before the chat turned sexual, and I opened myself up to a world where suddenly I had something to offer. Chat soon turned to pornography, where I was caught in a web I could not get out of.

Afraid I would eventually get caught by the college, I purchased my own computer for my bedroom at home, with my own Internet connection. My parents probably had no clue about what I was doing—I was a girl; surely women don't struggle with this type of thing, right? So began a cycle of an eleven-year addiction to pornography.

Many, many times I thought I could just quit. I would go to the front at church and get prayed for, hoping that God would just "heal" me from this instantly. Many Sundays I would go home thinking I was cured, but a few days later I would fall again. I felt many things—fear of being caught, shame for being a hypocrite

(I was in the choir at church and even on the youth staff), and that something was very wrong with me being a woman and having issues with something only men struggled with (or so I thought). I was afraid if anyone ever found out, I would lose everything.

It wasn't long before online pornography wasn't enough. I needed to be pursued and chased by men in a sexual way, so I gave myself away to anyone who showed even a remote interest in me and I did things I never thought I'd ever do in a million years. I even ended up with a pregnancy scare and a trip to Planned Parenthood. I took the morning-after pill to "erase" my mistake, but that wasn't even bottom enough for me.

My first rock bottom came one day a few years later after I was married. My three-year-old son walked in on me viewing porn. I hope to goodness he never saw anything, but it was enough to shake me to realize what kind of generational curse I was allowing to begin. My final bottom was when I was seven or eight months pregnant with my second son, and I was waking up in the middle of the night to view porn because I couldn't sleep without some kind of sexual release. I realized I could not live like this any longer.

The surrender finally came when my family and I changed churches and we started attending a church unlike any I'd been to before. This church encouraged being vulnerable, exposing your weaknesses, and was populated with a safe community of people who could literally "bear one another's burdens." I remember opening my mouth and actually saying it out loud to two different women in one weekend. What I couldn't believe was, *both* of them struggled with pornography addiction as well, and it was like the light of hope finally shone for the first time in my life. Someone else had this problem other than me? And they were both WOMEN?

I confessed to my husband as well, to which he replied that he had known for a long time (how, I don't know; I thought I had done well covering it up). He forgave me and completely supported me receiving help and sharing my story with others. If it wasn't for his unconditional love and support, I wouldn't be where I am today.

After claiming about two years of freedom, I came in contact with a wonderful ministry called Dirty Girls Ministries, where I was able to network with other women like me, receive encouragement and hope, and also begin to reach out to others to help them in their struggles. I learned that my journey of healing was only just beginning. Self-discipline + time = abstinence—but only abstinence. There was more to recover from than that. Real transformation occurred only after I realized that my heart needed to change too.

Over the last year, God has taken me on a journey to revisit old traumas from my past where I had checked out of owning my responsibility in the matter—my own feelings, thoughts, and beliefs about myself and others. Even though I wasn't "acting out" any longer, I turned off everything sexual and pretended it didn't exist. See, I was still trying to cope, but in the opposite direction of acting out; I was now acting in.

I'm still on a journey of healing in this area, and I always will be. But the difference is there is no more fear, there is no more shame or condemnation (Romans 8:1); and all the old beliefs I had about myself that were lies from the enemy Satan, I've replaced with the truths of God's Word . . . what He says about me, the hope that is mine for the taking, grace, redemption, and His divine love—which I never thought was really for me. "We demolish arguments and every pretension that sets itself up against the knowledge of God, and we take captive every thought to make it obedient to Christ" (2 Corinthians 10:5).

Dear sister reading my story, know there is hope for you. You are *not* alone; the silence has kept you prisoner for far too long. Fear and shame do not have to keep you bound any longer. There is so much grace and hope for you if you are willing to take God's hand and let Him begin to lead you down the road to recovery. I can promise you it's messy and hard, and it will not happen overnight, but joy and peace will come along the way and it will be more than you could ever imagine.

I pray that my story maybe has touched something in you that you can relate to, that you will feel an overwhelming love from your Creator, and that He will give you the strength to begin your journey right now with Him. I promise it's worth it; you are worth it.

Chapter 5

A-ACCOUNTABILITY:

Restoring Our Character

When professor and author Dallas Willard[6] was asked, "If a person wants to grow spiritually, where is a good place to start?" his answer was, "Do the next right thing you know you ought to do because that's what God wants you to do . . . But you will need help."

That is why accountability is such an important part of the healing process. Accountability in the form of a trusted friend, mentor, or spiritual authority.

But for most addicts, we really don't like the idea of being told what to do and how to do it. It is just our way as control freaks. In our own way we've been controlling our behavior for a long time, whether by controlling who knows about it or the careful covering of our tracks.

Unfortunately the reality, and what we have to begin to accept, is that we have no control. If we had control over any of it, it wouldn't have become an addiction.

So we need to hand the wheel over to someone else.

The road to freedom is paved in drastic measures. You have to do whatever it takes to put God and your desire for wholeness above all else.

Just like confession means talking about the elephant in the room, accountability is about allowing someone to help you fight the elephant.

And accountability is about accepting correction when we do relapse . . . and for most of us, a relapse will happen.

Accountability is about accepting correction when we do relapse . . . and for most of us, a relapse will happen.

Your mentor should be someone of your same gender and preferably (but not required) be someone who has a history of sexual addiction. Much like an AA sponsor, it helps to have accountability with someone who has experienced and found victory in this kind of addiction.

Pay It Forward

I have had the same accountability partner for eight years. She is the same woman who shared her story with me when I was at rock bottom. Our relationship works because we each understand where the other is coming from.

Her story began when she was sixteen years old. She grew up in a super-conservative atmosphere and didn't really understand a whole lot about sex. But she began to hear about it from kids in her high school. For her, she figured the best way to find out more was by looking on the Internet.

But she soon began to notice that she would want to go back to the computer and look at this stuff more. And it went from a curiosity she would satisfy once a week or so after her parents had gone to bed to a full-blown addiction. And she became more and more addicted, and more and more engrossed in this world.

So here she was, a pastor's kid, a good little Christian girl, totally addicted to porn. But when her online life started coming out into her offline life, she knew she had a problem. She decided she needed to get rid of her computer because to her it was the root of it all. It was where she talked to guys. It was where she did everything.

One night she had finally had enough. She unplugged her computer, picked it up, and walked it downstairs to the Dumpster outside her apartment. She said a little prayer of forgiveness asking God to forgive her for everything she had done.

And she thought that was enough to kick the addiction.

But even with her computer gone, she still had an addiction. The images in her mind and the way she would think about things were still haunting her. She was also completely overwhelmed with the shame that came with them.

Like me, she thought she could never talk to anybody about this because it had been her belief that it was totally natural for guys to look at porn or have sex. It's something that guys even celebrate sometimes, but for a girl to have an addiction like this? She felt she must have been the only one. A few years later, she met a friend who made it safe for her to confess, and they formed a relationship of accountability that lasted for several years.

She paid it forward when she did the same for me.

Drastic Measures

Throughout my addiction the Internet was my preferred source for pornography. So I had to take some big steps toward making sure I couldn't access porn or engage in porn-related activities while I used my computer.

Or any other computer for that matter.

First, I added accountability software that tracked my Internet activity at all times. Yes, things like that do exist (see pages 145–149 for resources).

If I ever viewed questionable content, my accountability partner would be notified via e-mail. This provided open and honest dialogue between us. I knew that if I were to view porn or do other questionable activities, she would know about it, and I would have no way of hiding.

Knowing someone would be seeing my Internet meanderings sure did make me think twice before clicking on something I shouldn't.

While I did not and do not use Internet filtering, I don't want to count it out as a very viable option. Filters are often way too easy to get around, and for me personally, they didn't promote growth in the area of self-discipline. My recommendation is and will always be personal responsibility over filtering only. If you are going to go the filtering route (some people need it), I highly encourage you to also use accountability software. It is added protection that in the event you do stumble, someone knows it.

Many other tough choices had to be made to ensure I was being held accountable.

I could also no longer be on my computer in private. If I used my computer, it was in the middle of a living space or in public. If working on my computer in private was absolutely necessary, my accountability partner would know ahead of time.

But even with all of these things in place, I was not always perfect.

A Sinner's Trifecta

Almost six years after I left pornography and my other sexual addictions behind, I slipped up.

I remember the rituals that began to unfold in my mind. The deep pangs of emotion that I was feeling in that moment were so strong I could taste them.

I had just returned home from a four-day whirlwind trip. I had gone from Kansas City to Los Angeles, to Las Vegas, back to LA, and finally returned to Kansas City.

I was stressed. I was exhausted. I was lonely. It was an addict's trifecta. Even for a recovering one.

Temptation
is not a sin . . . acting on your temptation is.

I remember the rituals that began to unfold in my mind. The deep pangs of emotion that I was feeling in that moment were so strong I could taste them. But instead of connecting with my accountability partner or doing a redirecting exercise or, more important, going to God . . . I chose to go against everything I knew to do . . . and went to the one thing that I knew would leave me most empty.

It wasn't pornography. But instead it was the one area that had been the most difficult for me to keep in check. Phone sex.

If I were ever going to slip up, it would have been with phone sex, because it was the one area I didn't have accountability in. No one in my life had access to my phone records, so I knew if I was going to do anything I could get away with it.

It ended as quickly as it began.

And it isn't something I've talked about, maybe to just one or two people since. And it isn't my intention to simply air my dirty laundry here.

But I share it today because it is something I hope you, the person who is striving for freedom, will read and learn from. That even when you think you have all of your bases covered, look again.

And I also share it because even though I slipped, I didn't allow the enemy to rob me of my mission and my call to begin my ministry. Which I see now is exactly what the enemy wanted to have happen. You see, this slipup occurred the same month I launched Dirty Girls Ministries.

But His grace is still sufficient, and His is power is made perfect in our weakness.

And today I have better defenses in place to protect myself in that vulnerable area.

Temptation never ends. It never does. And while temptation is not a sin . . . acting on your temptation is.

"Watch and pray so that you will not fall into temptation. The spirit is willing, but the body is weak" (Matthew 26:41).

The enemy is clever. He will use what he knows works to break you down. Having solid accountability in your life is nonnegotiable, as is having a trusting relationship with Jesus Christ. Those two things will be your life preserver when temptation comes.

Becoming clean

1. Have you found a mentor, friend, or someone to serve as a guide? Who is it? If you have not found one yet, pray that God will grant you the courage this week to ask someone to begin that relationship

2. Which area of your addiction do you feel will require the most drastic measure of discipline and accountability in order for you to achieve freedom? What ideas do you have that will help you achieve this?

3. What day of the week or time of day are you most tempted? What are some ways to adjust your routine so temptation is no longer standing between you and freedom.

4. Whether or not you currently have an accountability partner, you should begin establishing new boundaries and putting tools in place to help you take control of your behavior (e.g., Internet filtering, Internet accountability). See pages 146-147 for a list of great accountability resources. Before the day ends, explore this list and put one into place.

5. Psalm 103:2–5 says, "Praise the Lord, O my soul, and forget not all his benefits—who forgives all your sins and heals all your diseases, who redeems your life from the pit and crowns you with love and compassion, who satisfies your desires with good things so that your youth is renewed like the eagle's."

   What would it mean for you to have all your desires satisfied with good things and your youth renewed as promised in this passage?

Testimonial:
Charlotte Comes Clean

I was brought up in a fairly posh, English, middle-class, Christian family. I was happy, but I always felt different from others. I struggled to read and write at my age level, and I forgot what I learned moments later; I lost attention quickly. I would fall over nothing, and the list goes on.

My mother was a teacher and noticed. I was tested for dyslexia when I was six. It turned out I didn't just have dyslexia but also dyspraxia. I instantly felt like an outcast. People looked at me like I was different from other children, and treated me differently too.

When I was seven, my parents sent me to a special needs school. I loved it there. I felt normal. I began to learn how to read and write.

After only one year I switched schools and went to a boarding school. I was a day pupil there. School finished at six o'clock, and I had Saturday school also. I was bullied and ignored during my first two years there. Slowly I stopped being a part of my family. Finally in year five, I made a friend. I think it was around that time I also discovered pornography.

My older brother left a book in the bathroom. A smutty novel. At that time in my life I was scared of the dark. So one night I crept out of my bedroom and sat in the bathroom with the light on. I figured that if my parents woke up I wouldn't get scolded if it looked like I was on the toilet. I found the book, and to kill time, began to read it. It consumed me. I didn't understand it very well but it made me feel good. It seemed to fill a part of me that had been empty. I even started reading it during the day. One day my brother walked in and saw what I was reading. With anger and shock he took it from me and told me not to read it again. I respected and loved my brother, so I stopped.

In my junior year, I still felt incredibly lonely and depressed. School now lasted from 8:15a.m. to 9:00 p.m. I only went home to sleep. I was on the computer one day, wasting time, when I found it: a free pornography site. I began watching. The sense of relief was exhilarating. It made me feel loved and accepted for those ten minutes it was on. So I watched one clip after another.

Soon it was all I cared about.

The summer before my senior year, I went to Soul Survivor (a youth Christian conference). God found me and didn't judge me. I cried for three hours after I told someone about my addiction. It was agony, but such relief. I started praying. I found the Bible hard to read, but God began to give me spiritual gifts, and it got easier to understand. It's true what the Bible says—that God will use the least of us, the weakest.

But on the other side of things, I was slipping further into pornography. I was trying to fight it on my own, and I was losing.

I barely passed high school. However, I managed to get into a university, but I needed a break. So I decided to take a year off between school and university. I went to work with a Christian charity in Australia called YWAM (Youth With A Mission). Here they helped break down some more of my barriers. I even managed to tell them about my addiction. I felt safe and loved. I didn't look at pornography for six months.

The moment I returned home, I went right back to pornography. I couldn't cope on my own. So I pulled out of university and back to YWAM, but this time in the USA. Again I felt I could fight it there. I felt accepted. No judgment. Every now and then I would slip, but I would get back on my feet and try again the next day.

I was alone and friendless for most of my life, but I now see God's handprints all over my life. Protecting me, comforting me, loving me, and never leaving me, even when I felt like He had. It's hard to fight when you're by yourself, but with others you can go forward. I'm taking each day as it comes. Forgiving myself and others.

Chapter 6

R- RESPONSIBILITY:

Owning My Part of the Story

When I first began sharing about my pornography addiction, the relationship I had with my dad became an integral part of the story. I'd share elaborate tales of how he wasn't around for me.

How he wasn't around physically because his job always kept him traveling when I was growing up. How when he would be home, he wasn't around for me emotionally. How we never connected on any real level.

I really didn't know him, and he really didn't know me.

I'd share about how the void I had felt in not having a solid relationship with my dad was the sole reason I had done what I did. That he was the reason I even began looking at pornography, because of how it filled me with a false sense of intimacy, which was missing from my relationship with him.

Intimacy I wasn't receiving at home. Intimacy I wasn't receiving from him.

I threw a lot of blame his way for what I had done. Grasping and reaching for any excuse other than myself.

So, even as an adult, I used my dad's lack of involvement in my life as a cop-out or an excuse for my actions. Instead of taking responsibility for the choices I had outright made.

I've learned something over the years . . . that blaming others for my choices would not produce much change in me.

But I've learned something over the years . . . that blaming others for my choices would not produce much change in me.

In fact, it would keep me in a holding pattern. One that says that no matter what goes wrong in my life, no matter how screwed up things get, no matter how badly I mess something up . . . I could just blame someone else, and everything will turn out just fine.

We all know that doesn't work in real life, so it certainly won't work for this. Unless of course I wanted to remain in an emotional prison.

While some of the junk between my dad and me had a part in my story, owning my own part of the story is about taking responsibility for what I did do and even what I didn't do.

It meant looking deep inside myself and acknowledging where I had messed up. It meant having to suck it up and grow up.

I was well into year seven of my sobriety before I finally got up the nerve to tell my dad about my past.

Believe it or not, I had somehow achieved nearly sixteen years of secrecy. Sixteen years of keeping him in the dark about my behavior. Even while I was beginning to tell others in my family, like my mom, about my addiction, I would make sure my dad remained in the dark. Everyone else was sworn to secrecy. I made them believe it was because I wanted to be the one to tell him.

When in reality, I just wanted to keep control of the situation.

Remember our need as addicts to keep control? That control we actually don't have at all?

Keeping it secret from him while I was in addiction made sense. I kept it from everyone. But through several years of recovery and even as I began to counsel other women through their own addictions, I went to great lengths to remain in control.

All the while knowing that my dad just had to search my name on the Internet, and he would have been able to read my whole story. After all, I had launched a ministry, was already writing this book, and had been speaking about this topic for quite some time.

All the information was out there.

But I believe the Lord protected him from having to find out that way. I believe the Lord protected him from finding out from someone else. I believe God wanted me to have the opportunity to honor my dad instead of keeping him duped. I believe He wanted me to suck it up and face the music.

I was living in freedom from the bondage of my sexual addiction, but I was still in bondage to the fear of its exposure.

I could have gone another sixteen years and not have batted an eye, but it would still have been for wholly selfish reasons.

I had a lot of fear of how he was going to react (of what he would think of me, his only daughter, and telling him about my past meant I was finally going to take responsibility for my part of it (admit it was not all on him).

Out of Hiding

And that moment came on February 9, 2010.

I was leading yet another support group in my church, walking women through the process of confession and taking responsibility. Just like we're talking about in this chapter.

That night it was as though I heard it all for the first time.

While I wasn't still struggling in the area of addiction anymore, I was still hiding my past and hiding it in a pretty big way.

I was in direct disobedience by keeping my dad in the dark and not giving him the respect his position in my life required. I knew in my heart that I had not just another confession to make, but a pretty big opportunity to take responsibility.

Upon arriving home that night, I texted my dad a short message.

"If you're up, I need to talk to you about something."

If you knew my dad, you'd know that a message like that would shoot through him an immediate need to rescue me. While he wasn't around much, he always made me feel safe and was quick to take control of a situation.

It wasn't until the moment I told him that I finally felt free.

To make everything better.

He called, expecting to hear that something was wrong, and was ready to fix it.

But what he received was his daughter, his only daughter, on the other end of the phone, pouring out her heart to him for the very first time.

"Dad, I have something to tell you. Something that I have kept you in the dark about for a very long time. In fact, it is something I have lied about more than once because I was both too embarrassed and scared to admit it . . . As a teenager I had an addiction to pornography."

I'd never known my dad to be so helpless, but at the same time, so engaged. You could have heard a pin drop in between my words, my tears, and his silence.

My dad is not generally a silent type. But he allowed me to speak my piece.

And would you believe it? His reaction wasn't bad at all. In fact, in more ways than one he surprised me with his response to my confession. And in his own way actually commended me for having overcome my addiction and encouraged me in what I am trying to do now for others in ministry.

Being obedient is simply acting in response to what the Lord has already asked us to do.

Having my dad affirm not only me but also affirm the ministry that I was setting out to do did more for our relationship in that one moment than in all the moments we had before that.

It wasn't until the moment I told him that I finally felt free. Not only free to do ministry openly, but free from the secret I was still holding so tightly to.

Because even as I led women through recovery and had been doing all of these "good things," I was still constantly covering my tracks.

I was hiding the bad with the good.

Just as confession is an act of obedience, so is taking responsibility for what we have done. Don't shy away from obedience. Being obedient is simply acting in response to what the Lord has already asked us to do.

Read Luke 15:11–24. I've provided it here. But as you read it, replace the word "son" with "daughter" and see if you don't hear it a bit differently. Perhaps even see yourself in the story.

There was a man who had two sons. The younger one said to his father, "Father, give me my share of the estate." So he divided his property between them.

Not long after that, the younger son got together all he had, set off for a distant country and there squandered his wealth in wild living. After he had spent everything, there was a severe famine in that whole country, and he began to be in need. So he went and hired himself out to a citizen of that country, who sent him to his fields to feed pigs. He longed to fill his stomach with the pods that the pigs were eating, but no one gave him anything.

When he came to his senses, he said, "How many of my father's hired men have food to spare, and here I am starving to death! I will set out and go back to my father and say to him: Father, I have sinned against heaven and against you. I am no longer worthy to be called your son; make me like one of your hired men." So he got up and went to his father.

But while he was still a long way off, his father saw him and was filled with compassion for him; he ran to his son, threw his arms around him and kissed him.

The son said to him, "Father, I have sinned against heaven

103

and against you. I am no longer worthy to be called your son."
But the father said to his servants, "Quick! Bring the best robe and put it on him. Put a ring on his finger and sandals on his feet. Bring the fattened calf and kill it. Let's have a feast and celebrate. For this son of mine was dead and is alive again; he was lost and is found." So they began to celebrate.

A ring? A feast? A celebration? What?

That dude completely embarrassed his family.

In the culture in which this story is set, a boy asking his father for his inheritance before his death would be equal to him telling his father to die.

It would have been grounds for execution.

But because his father loved his son, he gave him what he asked for.

And yet the son squandered it all.

He spent every dime on whores and gambling.

He eventually was left with nothing and was forced to work by feeding pigs.

Since he was starving, even the pigs' food was appealing to him.

Imagine.

A Jewish man forced to care after pigs and even desiring to eat after them.

There was no lower point this guy could have gone.

He knew he had done something irreversible to his father.

But he also knew that he couldn't get any lower. That at least if he went home and took responsibility for the actions he'd done that maybe, just maybe, his father would hire him as a servant.

You know how the story ends.

His father welcomed him home with open arms.

Just thankful to have his son back home.

Taking responsibility for our less than desirable actions is not only obedient, but it is usually welcomed with a much better response than we often expect.

Becoming clean

1. List some ways you have avoided taking responsibility for your past behaviors and how doing so may have harmed others, directly or indirectly.

2. Create a personal inventory of those your actions have harmed.
   - Write down their names. Whether the harm was physical, emotional, spiritual, or even financial—acknowledge who was hurt during the warpath of your addiction.
   - Next to each name, describe what it is you desire, taking responsibility for things such as the opportunities you missed because of time you spent acting out, the lies you told in order to hide your behavior, two-facedness you showed as a Christian, and so on. (Remember that the point of this exercise is not to fill you with shame or regret. Ask God to fill you with the peace of His grace as you create this inventory.)

3. Taking responsibility isn't about manipulation or making yourself feel better. Taking responsibility is about saying, "I'm sorry," with humility and without the expectation of receiving forgiveness. Journal about your reasons for wanting to take responsibility in each case. Pray for God to grant you discernment for your next steps.

4. Develop a plan for taking responsibility. How will you approach these people? However, do not take any next steps without first sharing your plan with your accountability partner or support group.

5. Philippians 1:6 says, " . . . being confident of this, that he who began a good work in you will carry it on to completion until the day of Christ Jesus." Consider the good work God wants to do in you through your obedience in taking responsibility.

Testimonial:
Jennifer Comes Clean

I don't really know when my addiction started; as long as I can remember, I have been drawn to sex and lust. It started with imagination and curiosity, and grew to desire and acting out. I was first exposed to porn at my dad's work, where his coworkers displayed pictures of women at their workstations. I remember specifically telling myself that I couldn't wait until I was older and could look at porn.

For six years I had this deep dark secret that I hid from everyone. I thought I was the only girl in the world who had this problem and if anyone ever found out they would think I was a freak. I would sneak onto the Internet and look at porn; my mind was completely out of control with lust. I even crashed my work computer trying to cover up my secret life and cost the business thousands of dollars to repair it; they never found out. My life felt like walls closing in, and I couldn't last much longer with this secret.

In my freshman year in college I got a phone call from my good friend. She was crying uncontrollably. She explained to me that she had been struggling for years with sexual addiction and needed my help. What freedom I felt at that moment! I told her I had been struggling too, and we began to hold each other accountable and encourage each other through the hard times.

During those years, I met many girls who were also struggling with sexual sin, many of whom would join us in our fight to break this bondage. Eventually my friend and I went on to intern in different ministries in different states, and I continued to grow and become stronger. When I came back home, however, she was gone and I found I had no one to hold me accountable and that I hadn't really "fixed" anything.

I fell back even harder into my habits, blaming my past, or God, or even my mentor. I wanted desperately to be free, to know why God gave me this struggle. I dragged people down with me.

I always held to the belief that God made me special for someone and that he was worth waiting for. I hated what this addiction was doing to me; I felt like I was living a double life and was slowly being torn down the middle. I hated that I liked the feeling it gave me, I hated the guilt and condemnation that came with my failure, and eventually I confessed to my closest friends and mentors that I had slipped up again.

I became so sick of struggling that I finally sought out help and even got the strength and courage to join a support group for women. I realized that I'd already come very far in my journey to freedom compared to the ladies I saw who were just starting out.

I've always appreciated people who fight for what they want, who crawl through the desert to get to the well; they always learn more, stand taller and stronger than those who can do an instantaneous turnabout. It's like going on a diet versus a lifestyle change; a diet will get you fast results but rarely has long-lasting effects. A lifestyle change requires you to take time to look at your bad habits and poor choices, and completely change what you do for the rest of your life so that you don't go back to your destructive habits.

That's where I'm at. I may not be completely over my battle, but I am making tough choices that will benefit me for the rest of my life. God tells me that He has a plan and purpose for my life, not to harm me, but to prosper me (see Jeremiah 29:11). The enemy has come to destroy me, but God says He can take that and use it for good. I have a hope that my story and my struggle will inspire and influence other women to seek out the same freedom.

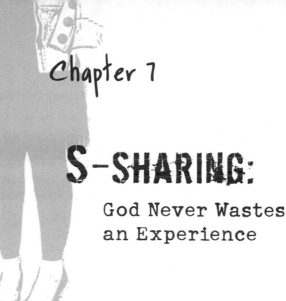

Chapter 7

S-SHARING:

God Never Wastes an Experience

It would be five years into my journey before I'd begin to really talk about it.

"Hey, thanks, Jesus, and now let's never talk about it again" was my philosophy on the whole thing.

What I had overcome was huge, and I was beyond thankful to God for His healing power and His grace in seeing me through it. But it was not my plan to write this book. It was certainly not my plan to form Dirty Girls Ministries.

Who was I to share my story? I was just a girl from Kansas who went through some junk and lived to tell about it.

Wait, lived to tell about it?

Yes, because it is a good story. Not because of who I am or what I did, but because of what God did.

People love a good redemption story. The very fact that I can sit here writing this book today is a testament to that fact.

And the more hopeless or messier the story, the more people like it. Cinderella. Frodo and Sam. Rudy. Helen Keller. Forrest Gump.

All household names. All stories that tell hopeless tales that appeared to be over before they really began. Yet all end with beautiful and hopeful redemption.

I believe God loves stories like these as well.

He Called Her Daughter

And the one I want to share is the story of the woman with the issue of blood from the book of Luke. To set the story, Jesus had been on His way to a man's home to save his daughter who was dying, but was stopped when another need presented itself.

As Jesus was on his way, the crowds almost crushed him. And a woman was there who had been subject to bleeding for twelve years, but no one could heal her. She came up behind him and touched the edge of his cloak, and immediately her bleeding stopped.

"Who touched me?" Jesus asked.

When they all denied it, Peter said, "Master, the people are crowding and pressing against you."

But Jesus said, "Someone touched me; I know that power has gone out from me."

Then the woman, seeing that she could not go unnoticed, came trembling and fell at his feet. In the presence of all the people, she told why she had touched him and how she had been instantly healed.

Then he said to her, "Daughter, your faith has healed you. Go in peace." (Luke 8:42–47)

If anyone had a story to tell it was this woman. But it was not one she cared to share in public.

She had been "subject to bleeding for twelve years." She bled in the way you would imagine a woman to bleed.

As a woman reading this, can you imagine the embarrassment and shame she endured on a daily basis?[7]

She'd likely spent every dime she had seeing physician after physician, yet no one was able to find a reason for her relentless bleeding.

She was desperate for the healing of her broken heart caused by the years of shame and isolation.

She'd given up all hope of ever being healed.

But then she heard about Jesus and the miracles He had been performing. In a final act of desperation, she knew she had to go to Him.

A woman bleeding during her cycle was deemed ritually unclean in this day and was to remain home for the five to seven days a month. But for this woman it had been twelve years since she had been able to live a normal life.

She took a chance when she heard Jesus was nearby. And as she made her way through the crowd of people, she carried with her much more than her ailment.

She also carried fear, loneliness, and disgrace. Her emotional hurts and scars were far worse than her physical ones.

The crowd was huge. It was a miracle she even reached Jesus. When the woman grabbed the hem of His robe, it was an act of desperation. She didn't know that by simply touching Him, that she'd be healed and yet she reached out. She was desperate for the healing of her body, yes. But more so: she was desperate for the healing of her broken heart caused by the years of shame and isolation she'd experienced. We all have hurts like these. Hurts that go way beyond the surface.

Immediately, she was healed.

Jesus turned around and faced the crowd to ask, "Who touched me?"

She told Him why she had touched Him and how she had been instantly healed. Jesus didn't need her to tell her story. He already knew what had happened.

Remember, Jesus had been on His way to heal a dying girl when He stopped to heal this woman. And yet the crowd was yelling and urging He to leave and get to the little girl's house—in fear that she would soon die. But He stopped in the middle of all the chaos around Him so that this woman could finally be heard.

It was as if the whole world stopped to face this woman in that moment.

When she finished talking, He responded by calling her "Daughter". It's the only time I can find that He ever called a woman "daughter." And He said it to this woman who had been a virtual outcast for twelve years.

As Jesus looked at this woman, He saw who she was always meant to be. Not her ailment or her scars. He saw the life she had been missing and He wanted to redeem it.

For the first time in twelve years, this woman knew what it felt like to be loved.

Good story, huh?

However, the greatest healing isn't the miraculous cure of her incurable disease. It was the healing of her heart.

If healing her body was all that He cared about, He wouldn't have stopped, turned around, asked the question. He wouldn't have looked straight at her, talked to her, listened.

But He did all those things. He wanted to let her talk.

To tell her story.

He wanted to call her Daughter.

He wanted to heal more than her body.

His wanted to heal her heart.

If He had just healed her body and left her to still carry the hurt from her twelve years of rejection and disgrace, nothing probably would have changed about the way she lived her life. She would have been the same shamed girl she had been for twelve years. Still dragging her bag of shame behind her. When Jesus looked at this woman, He saw who she was always meant to be. Not her ailment or her scars. He saw the life she had been missing and He wanted to redeem it.

And your healing won't be the miraculous recovery from your addiction.

It will be the healing of your heart.

When we have the opportunity to share our story, the greater is the healing that takes place within us. It breaks down our walls and our self-inflicted defenses. It allows love to come back into our lives.

I have a feeling that the woman who was healed never stopped proclaiming what had happened to her. Not just to her body, but what happened to her heart.

We've all experienced things in our lives that have fundamentally changed who we are. Some things have catapulted us toward the cross, while other things may have caused us to stray or become silent.

Healing comes from sharing those stories.

Because God never wastes an experience. He has plans for what you've been through. He intends to use your story.

You just need to start sharing it.

And we as the church need to be ready to listen.

Becoming clean

1. Begin writing your story. Keep it short and to the point. The following guidelines may come in handy as you write:

   - Describe what your addiction was made up of, your attempts at self-control, and any consequences you faced because of it.
   - Describe your rock-bottom experience, and what your healing journey has been like.
   - Describe how your life has changed now that you are free from your addiction and the thankfulness you have for God's grace.

2. Share your story with your accountability partner or support group. Ask for their feedback and rewrite your story as necessary.

3. List the names of three or four people who may also need to hear your story (those struggling, friends, family members, and so on). Keep a journal for the times you share, and describe their reactions.

4. Write a thank-you letter to those who have been an encouragement and support to you during your healing process.

5. First Corinthians 15:55–58 says, "'Where, O death, is your victory? Where, O death, is your sting?' The sting of death is sin, and the power of sin is the law. But thanks be to God! He gives us the victory through our Lord Jesus Christ. Therefore, my dear [sisters], stand firm. Let nothing move you. Always give yourselves fully to the work of the Lord, because you know that your labor in the Lord is not in vain."

   Consider what it means for you to give yourself fully to the work of God and how your story may be the catalyst for you to use.

Testimonial:
Stephanie Comes Clean

Twenty years. For twenty years I hid sin in my heart. Looking back, it's hard to believe it has been that long. How did I walk through two-thirds of my life without telling a soul about my deep, dark secret? Satan had filled me with such shame and guilt that I felt trapped. Trapped into doing everything I could to give the appearance of being a "perfect Christian" while attempting to hide my growing struggle with porn.

It started innocently. I was raised in a staunchly legalistic church in rural America where sex was a taboo topic. My parents never had a single conversation with me about sex, which left me to find the information on my own.

I can remember the moment perfectly. I was in middle school, and after hearing several friends make comments about sex, I knew I had to find out what it was. Like the "perfect" student I was, I went to the school library and headed straight to the health encyclopedias. What I read and saw captivated me. I was instantly hooked. When I checked that book out that very day and secretly looked at the pages at home, I felt like I was connecting to something. Had I known where it would have led me, I would have fled.

From that point, my growing curiosity got the best of me. In my teen years, I spent hours in the city library eagerly scanning romance novels only to read the dirty sections. I browsed health books desperately trying to find any visuals I could. Because I was working so hard to maintain my good girl image on the outside, I did everything to maintain my craving without being caught. How could the sweet girl in the youth group also be harboring a desire for porn?

The Internet took me to a whole new level. In college I could view pictures, videos, and stories in the privacy of my own room. Throughout my twenties I would go in cycles of spending entire weekends looking at porn to being so ridden with guilt I would stay away from it for weeks, only to be lured back. Sadly, as I spent more and more time looking at porn, the more my addiction needed to be fed. Finally, the visuals were no longer working. I yearned to experience what I saw. I didn't just crave the visual, I craved the physical. I was in my late twenties, still single, and angry at God because He hadn't provided a husband to fulfill my desires. I decided it was time to satisfy my cravings. And I became willing to do whatever it took to get it.

One night when I was feeling particularly out of control, I quickly placed an ad on Craigslist looking for a sexual partner. I knew all the risks involved, but my desire pushed me there, and Satan assured me I wouldn't become a news story. The response was overwhelming. It gave me confidence, power, and the feeling I was desired. I picked one man, corresponded with him, and, a few days later, met him. We slept together that night.

I kept that relationship for two years. I knew it wasn't going anywhere relationally. I balanced my life by sleeping at his place on Saturday night and waking up in time to go to church Sunday morning, with a smile on my face and my Bible in hand.

Finally, I could no longer keep both worlds going. It was too much work, and I was depressed. I was sure God's grace no longer applied to me, so I kept giving in to my desires. Yet, I knew there was something better for me.

I was in weekly counseling for an entire year before I could confess that I used porn. I could tell my counselor about the relationship I was in, but there was too much shame to tell her how I had gotten to that point. I thought it was bad enough that I was sleeping with a man outside of marriage. How could I ever open up about the grip porn had on me?

At the age of thirty-one, nearly twenty years after opening that library book for the first time, I told my counselor about my journey. Even though I greatly respected and trusted her, it was the most difficult thing I had ever talked about. I held back nothing for fear if it didn't come out that day, it never would. With tears in her eyes, my counselor thanked me, prayed for me, and assured me the blood of Christ covered every single sin in my life. And He still loved me. I felt a freedom I hadn't ever felt before that day. My secret was finally out.

That was nearly six months ago. My wonderful counselor came alongside me and asked me tough questions. I decided to do whatever it took, which included going to an intensive counseling workshop. I began to understand why I had become addicted to porn and what I needed to do to get out of it.

At the time I write this, I have been free for five months. It hasn't been easy. I'm learning to take God's promises of grace and love to heart, and attempting to forgive myself for my actions. I'm thankful for how God has worked in me. Five months ago I couldn't tell anyone about the hold porn had on me. Today, I'm involved in a recovery group and actively sharing my story. All the glory goes to God, as it is He alone who has gotten me to where I am today. I pray He will keep me strong, and in the moments I am weak, I pray I will lean on His strength. God can turn our messes into a message. I'm grateful He's doing that with me.

Chapter 8

IT IS FOR FREEDOM

You made it to the end of the book.

Good for you.

But how do you feel?

If you are like me, you probably don't feel much different from when you first picked up this book. Or you may even feel worse because you still haven't achieved any level of freedom.

And that's okay.

It is called "a process" for a reason. Because it is a process.

The temptation to act out never really goes away. But it is through the SCARS steps of healing and, more importantly, through Jesus that we can find our way back on track. These steps are not to be taken once or even just twice, but repeatedly throughout your journey.

This may mean getting to the end of this book and immediately begin reading it again.

We'll all screw up along the way, but having the grace to accept when those failures come and to move on and to grow and to learn from them, it is so important. And the freedom that comes from living a life of no secrets is something I wouldn't trade for the world.

What is liberating is taking back ownership of what we see, what we hear, and what we do.

From *Roe v. Wade* to lesbianism to birth control, women's liberation movements have made it their platform to give women a right over their own bodies.

Some good and some not so good have come out if it. But fast-forward to today, and we see that women are once again in a fight for liberation.

But this time, it is a personal fight and one that is more often fought all alone. In the last ten years especially, our culture of sexually provocative advertising and media have aided in the transformation of women from sexually submissive into sexually aggressive . . . and sexually obsessed.

As such, this is resulting in a rapidly growing addiction to pornography and sexual promiscuity among women today.

An article was written about me, groups I lead, Dirty Girls

Ministries, and this whole issue of women's addiction to pornography.

It struck a chord (or a nerve rather) and left some people saying, "Is this Crystal Renaud an antifeminist? Masturbation, sexual exploration, and pornography use is normal. She is setting women's lib back a hundred years."

But questions and statements like these could not be further from the truth. What is liberating about a woman being in bondage to her own perverse sexuality?

Nothing.

I know the bondage of pornography and compulsive sexual behavior firsthand, as I spent eight years of my own life in this addiction.

And what is liberating is taking back ownership of what we see, what we hear, and what we do. And as a result, living lives free from the things that can keep us in bondage.

That, my sweet sisters, is liberation.

Liberation that only biblical sexual wholeness can provide you.

"It is for freedom that Christ has set us free. Stand firm, then, and do not let yourselves be burdened again by a yoke of slavery" (Galatians 5:1).

PERSONAL INVENTORY

For Those Seeking
Freedom from Porn

Answer the following questions as they relate to your present use of pornography and engagement in sexual activity. It is imperative that you answer the questions honestly to the best of your ability.

Marital Status:

a) Single	c) Divorced
b) Married	d) Widowed

Current Age Bracket:

a) Under 18	d) 35–44
b) 18–24	e) 45+
c) 25–34	

At what age did you begin viewing pornography?

    a) 10 years old or younger

    b) 11–18

    c) 18+

Briefly describe how you first came in contact with pornography.

How did you feel when you were first exposed to pornography?

How long after your first exposure to pornography did you view it again?

    a) Hours later   d) A year later

    b) Days later   e) More than a year later

    c) Months later

Why did you go back to pornography after your first exposure to it?

How long have you now been viewing pornography?

    a) Under 1 year   c) 5–10 years

    b) 1–5 years

How many hours a week do you view pornography?

    a) Less than 5   c) 12–24

    b) 5–11   d) 24+

What forms of pornography do you view? (Choose all that apply.)

a) Internet

b) Magazines

c) Movies (R-rated or greater)

d) Strip clubs/peep shows

e) Erotica novels

f) Video games/animation

g) Other _____

h) All of the above

What is your reason for viewing pornography?

a) Physical release (masturbation, etc.)

b) Emotional release (fantasy, escape)

c) Spousal request

d) Other _____

How does pornography make you feel now that you've been viewing it over a longer period of time?

Have you ever promised yourself that you would never again view pornography?

What is the longest period of time that you have gone without viewing pornography in the last year?

a) 8 months to a year

b) 6–8 months

c) 4–6 months

d) 2–4 months

e) 1–2 months

f) 2 weeks to 1 month

g) 1 week

h) 1 or 2 days

After a period of abstinence what ultimately brings you back to pornography?

Have you viewed pornography while at school and/or work?

Have you lost a job or risked losing a job because of viewing of pornography?

Have you paid for pornography?

Have you accumulated debt from paying for pornography?

Do you risk legal problems in order to view pornography?
If yes, please describe.

Is your sexual addiction limited to pornography and/or masturbation?
If no, in what other areas is your sexual addiction personified?

Do you sometimes think that you are the only woman who has certain sexual thoughts or engages in certain sexual behaviors?

Does viewing pornography ever lead you to question your sexual orientation?

If yes, have you ever acted out physically with a member of the same sex as you?

If yes, briefly describe what led up to you having that experience. Do not describe the encounter.

Do you have close friends/relationships?

Has an important relationship been affected in a negative way or ended because of your inability to stop looking at pornography?

If yes, briefly describe.

Have you told anyone about your pornography addiction?

If yes, whom did you tell?

What was that person's reaction to your confession?

If married, does your husband know about your porn addiction?

If married, does your husband also struggle with a pornography addiction?

Do you have a mentor, accountability partner, or guide?

If yes, have you ever lied or not told the whole truth to your accountability partner regarding your behaviors?

Other than another person, do you have other forms of accountability (e.g., Internet filters)?

Have you ever been sexually abused?

If yes, have you told anyone about your abuse?

Briefly describe your family/home life while growing up.

Are there memories from your childhood that cause you pain? Briefly describe.

Do you suffer from any of the following?

a) Depression   d) Post-Traumatic Stress Disorder (PTSD)

b) Anxiety   e) Other _____

c) Insomnia

How long have you been suffering from one or more of these? When did you first notice the symptoms?

Are you currently on medication for one or more of the above?

If yes, how is the medication helping?

Personal Inventory: For Those Seeking Freedom from Porn

Have you ever sought counseling for one of more of these illnesses or specifically for your pornography addiction?
If yes, briefly describe your experience with counseling.

Does your sexual addiction interfere with your relationship with God?
If yes, please describe.

Do you consistently attend church/worship services or Bible study? Do you participate in daily quiet time and prayer?

Does your church have support groups for pornography addiction, and/or has it ever specifically discussed pornography in a sermon/message?

On a scale of 1 to 10 (10 being most severe), how would you personally rank the severity of your pornography addiction today?

1   2   3   4   5   6   7   8   9   10

For group use: Based on what you've shared with your group members, on a scale of 1 to 10 (10 being most severe), ask your group members to rank the severity of your pornography addiction today. What is the result?

1   2   3   4   5   6   7   8   9   10

Remember that no self-test can absolutely and accurately determine the nature of your problem or the solution. Please use it as a marker to help guide you along your own path. This is simply a screening device that can be helpful in deciding whether you need help or not. Feelings of concern, shame, or fear created by answering these questions may indicate the need to contact a professional for guidance. Based on your responses, you may benefit by seeking help from appropriate resources such as a professional knowledgeable about addiction, and/or joining a support group.

PERSONAL INVENTORY

For Those (mostly) Free from Porn

Answer the following questions as they relate to your past use of pornography and engagement in sexual activity. It is imperative that you answer the questions honestly to the best of your ability.

Marital Status:

a) Single	c) Divorced
b) Married	d) Widowed

Current Age Bracket:

a) Under 18	d) 35–44
b) 18–24	e) 45+
c) 25–34	

On a scale of 1 to 10 (10 being most severe), how would you personally rank the severity of your pornography addiction prior to your present stage of freedom?

1   2   3   4   5   6   7   8   9   10

At what age did you begin viewing pornography?
- a) 10 or younger
- b) 11–18
- c) 18+

Briefly describe how you were first exposed to pornography.

How did you feel when you were first exposed to pornography?

How long after your first exposure to pornography did you view it again?
- a) Hours later
- b) Days later
- c) Months later
- d) A year later
- e) More than a year later

Why did you go back to pornography after your first exposure to it?

How long did your pornography addiction last?
- a) Under 1 year
- b) 1–5 years
- c) 5–10 years
- d) 11+ years

How many hours a week did you view pornography?

    a) Less than 5   c) 12–24

    b) 5–11   d) 24+

What forms of pornography did you view? (Choose all that apply)

    a) Internet   e) Erotica novels

    b) Magazines   f) Video games/Animation

    c) Movies (R rated or greater)   h) All of the above

    d) Strip clubs/Peep shows   g) Other _____

What was your reason for viewing pornography?

    a) Physical release (masturbation, etc.)   c) Spousal request

    b) Emotional release (fantasy, escape)   d) Other _____

How did pornography make you feel after you had been viewing it over a longer period of time?

What was the longest period of time that you had gone without viewing pornography prior to your present stage of sobriety?

    a) 8 months to a year   e) 1–2 months

    b) 6–8 months   f) 2 weeks to 1 month

    c) 4–6 months   g) 1 week

    d) 2–4 months   h) 1 or 2 days

After any period of freedom, what ultimately brought you back to pornography?

Had you ever viewed pornography while at school and/or work?

Had you ever lost a job or risked losing a job because of viewing of pornography?

Had you ever paid for pornography?

Had you accumulated debt from paying for pornography?
If yes, are you still paying off your financial debt?

Did you risk legal problems in order to view pornography?
If yes, please describe.

Was your sexual addiction limited to pornography and/or masturbation?
If no, in what other areas did your sexual addiction present itself?

Did you sometimes think that you were the only woman who had certain sexual thoughts or engaged in certain sexual behaviors?

Did viewing pornography ever lead you to question your sexual orientation?
If yes, have you ever acted out physically with a member of the same sex as you?

If yes, briefly describe what led up to you having that experience. Do not describe the encounter.

Did you have close friends/relationships during your pornography addiction?

Did an important relationship in your life end because of your inability to stop looking at pornography?
If yes, briefly describe.

Have you told anyone about your pornography addiction?
If yes, whom did you tell?

What was the person's reaction to your confession?

If married, does your husband know about your porn addiction?

If married, does/did your husband also struggle with a pornography addiction?

Briefly describe how you overcame your pornography addiction.

How long has it been since you last viewed pornography?
- a) 30 days or less
- d) 2–5 years
- b) 1–6 months
- e) 5+ years
- c) 6–24 months

Are you still tempted to view pornography?

If so, what necessary steps do you take to remain sober?

What sexual behavior has been the most for you difficult to stop?

Do you fear relapsing?

Do you have an accountability partner, mentor, or guide?
If yes, have you ever lied or not told the whole truth to your mentor regarding your behaviors?

Other than another person, do you have other forms of accountability (e.g., Internet filters)?

Have you ever been sexually abused?
If yes, have you told anyone about your abuse?

Briefly describe your family/home life while growing up.

Personal Inventory: For Those (mostly) Free from Porn

Are there memories from your childhood that cause you pain? Briefly describe.

Do you suffer from any of the following?
- a) Depression
- b) Anxiety
- c) Insomnia
- d) Post-Traumatic Stress Disorder (PTSD)
- e) Other _____

How long have you been suffering from one or more of these? When did you first notice the symptoms?

Are you currently on medication for one or more of the above?
If yes, how is the medication helping?

Have you ever sought counseling for one of more of these illnesses or specifically for your pornography addiction?
If yes, briefly describe your experience with counseling.

Did your sexual addiction interfere with your relationship with God?
If yes, please describe.

During your addiction, did you consistently attend church/worship services or Bible study? Did you participate in daily quiet time and prayer?

Does your church have support groups for pornography addiction, and/or has it ever specifically discussed pornography in a sermon/message?

On a scale of 1 to 10 (10 being most severe), how would you personally rank the severity of your pornography addiction today?

1   2   3   4   5   6   7   8   9   10

For group use: Based on what you've shared with your group members, on a scale of 1 to 10 (10 being most severe), ask your group members to rank the severity of your pornography addiction today. What is the result?

1   2   3   4   5   6   7   8   9   10

Remember that no self-test can absolutely and accurately determine the nature of your problem or the solution. Please use it as a marker to help guide you along your own path. This is simply a screening device that can be helpful in deciding whether you need help or not. Feelings of concern, shame, or fear created by answering these questions may indicate the need to contact a professional for guidance. Based on your responses, you may benefit by seeking help from appropriate resources, such as a professional knowledgeable about addiction, and/or joining a support group.

The Twelve Steps of Sexaholics Anonymous

1. We admitted that we were powerless over lust—that our lives had become unmanageable.

2. Came to believe that a Power* greater than ourselves could restore us to sanity.

3. Made a decision to turn our will and our lives over to the care of God as we understand Him.*

4. Made a searching and fearless moral inventory of ourselves.

5. Admitted to God, to ourselves, and to another human being the exact nature of our wrongs.

6. Were entirely ready to have God remove all these defects of character.

7. Humbly asked Him to remove our shortcomings.

8. Made a list of all persons we had harmed, and became willing to make amends to them all.

9. Made direct amends to such people wherever possible, except when to do so would injure them or others.

10. Continued to take personal inventory, and when we were wrong, promptly admitted it.

11. Sought through prayer and meditation to improve our conscious contact with God as we understood Him,* praying only for knowledge of His will for us and the power to carry that out.

12. Having had a spiritual awakening as the result of these steps, we tried to carry this message to sexaholics and to practice these principles in all our affairs.

*As Christians, we do not look to a higher power, but believe that God has revealed Himself in the Bible, His Word; we believe in Jesus Christ as His only Son. He is our Savior, the only One who can redeem lives.

CRYSTAL RENAUD

and Dirty Girls
Ministries

Crystal Renaud is founder and executive director of Dirty Girls Ministries, a not-for-profit ministry helping women struggling with pornography and sexual addiction.

Founded by Crystal in February 2009, the desire of Dirty Girls Ministries is to break through the stigmatic barriers that are keeping women in bondage to this addiction. DGM promotes open and honest conversation through accountability, online community, recovery groups, networking opportunities for churches, addiction awareness, and more.

Crystal has used the experience gained from her own pornography addiction to counsel hundreds of women. She writes and speaks in various venues on the topic. She also holds a certification in sexual addiction counseling from the American Association of

Christian Counselors. Crystal is single and resides in the Kansas City area.

Contact Crystal Renaud or Dirty Girls Ministries:
Website: http://dirtygirlsministries.com
Booking: booking@dirtygirlsministries.com
Email: info@dirtygirlsministries.com
Twitter: http://twitter.com/crystalrenaud
Facebook: http://facebook.com/dirtygirlsmin

RESOURCES

Because resources update often, please visit the resource section of Dirty Girls Ministries' website (http://dirtygirlsministries .com) for a current list.

Online Accountability
Covenant Eyes from CovenantEyes.com

The Covenant Eyes Accountability Service monitors every website you visit and rates those sites for objectionable content. An easy-to-read report is regularly e-mailed to the accountability partner you choose. This enables you to be transparent with trusted friends or mentors about the temptations you face and the choices you make online. These weekly reports help you build a new connection with your friend and allow you to have deep and intimate conversations in your walk toward purity.

The Accountability Service is available for Windows, Mac, and a growing number of handheld devices, including iPhone, iPod touch, and iPad at http://www.CovenantEyes.com.

X3Watch from XXXChurch.com

X3Watch is an accountability software program that helps with online integrity. Whenever you browse the Internet and access a site that may contain questionable material, the program will record the site name, time, and date the site was visited. A person of your choice (an accountability partner) will receive an e-mail containing all possible questionable sites you may have visited within the month. This information is meant to encourage open and honest conversation between friends and help us all be more accountable. Get X3Watch for PC, Mac, iPhone, iPad, iTouch, and Android at http://www.xxxchurch.com.

X3Pure from XXXChurch.com

The objective of the X3Pure project is to enable a speedy and effective recovery for men and women dealing with pornography and other sex-related addictions in the most confidential and professional manner possible. X3Pure is the first online, confidential, streaming-video solution for dealing with pornography addiction. This powerful workshop helps you take each important step toward recovery from your pornography addiction and is accessible from any Internet-connected computer at any time. X3Pure includes a copy of Safe Eyes software that is good for up to three computers. For more information about the X3Pure visit http://www.xxx church.com.

Books

Ferree, Marnie. *No Stones: Women Redeemed from Sexual Addiction*. Downers Grove, IL, InterVarsity Press, 2010.

Jackson, Anne. *Permission to Speak Freely: Essays and Art on Confession, Grace, and Fear*. Nashville, Thomas Nelson, 2010.

Jones, Stan and Brenna Jones, God's Design for Sex series. *The Story of Me* (ages 3–5); *Before I Was Born* (ages 5–8); *What's the Big Deal?* (ages 8–11); *Facing the Facts: The Truth about Sex and You* (ages 11–14). Colorado Springs, NavPress, 2007.

Laaser, Mark. *Healing the Wounds of Sexual Addiction*. Grand Rapids, Zondervan, 2004.

Resources for Locating Recovery Groups

Bethesda Workshops: www.bethesdaworkshops.org
Dirty Girls Ministries: www.dirtygirlsministries.com
L.I.F.E. Ministries: www.freedomeveryday.org
pureHOPE: www.purehope.net
Pure Life Alliance: www.purelifealliance.org
Pure Life Ministries: www.purelifeministries.org

Setting Captives Free: www.settingcaptivesfree.com
Sexaholics Anonymous: www.sa.org

Blogs of Others Coming Clean

Jenni Clayville, www.jenniclayville.com
Justin and Trisha Davis, www.refineus.org
Anne Jackson, www.annejacksonwrites.com
Alece Ronzino, www.gritandglory.com
Sarah Markley, www.sarahmarkley.com
Nicole Wick, www.nicolewick.com

Notes

1. Ramona Richards, "Dirty Little Secret: Men Aren't the Only Ones Lured by Internet Porn," *Today's Christian Woman*, 2003, September/October, vol. 25, issue 5: 58.

2. http://internet-filter-review.toptenreviews.com/internet-pornography-statistics.html.

3. http://www.sa.org/steps.php.

4. Marnie Ferree, *L.I.F.E. Guide for Women*, Freedom Everyday LLC, 2007, 148.

5. A. W. Tozer, *The Attributes of God* volume 1 and *The Attributes of God* volume 2 (Camp Hill, PA: WingSpread Publishers, 2007).

6. Dallas Willard is a professor in the School of Philosophy at the University of Southern California in Los Angeles, a speaker, and the author of numerous books such as *The Divine Conspiracy* and *Knowing Christ Today*.

7. See www.gritandglory.com/2007/09/14/the-hem-of-his-robe http://www.gritandglory.com/2007/09/14/the-hem-of-his-robe and www.womeninthebible.net/2.6.Menstruating_woman.htmhttp://www. womeninthebible.net/2.6.Menstruating_woman.htm for more insight into this woman's story.

ACKNOWLEDGMENTS

Writing this book has been one of the most challenging and yet rewarding experiences of my life. It has stretched me beyond what I thought I could handle and for that I will be forever grateful for this experience.

I will also be forever grateful to all the people who stood by me, supported me, and were even a bit neglected by me while I was writing this labor of love. And also to those who have played a part in shaping me into the person I am today. I couldn't possibly name you all, but whether you are mentioned by name or not, this book would not exist without you.

To my mom, Gina, and my sister, Emily, for how you love me at my crabbiest moments. When I wanted to give up and close the book on this book, thank you for giving me the encouragement I needed to keep going. I love you.

To my friends who are like another family to me and who have bettered by life by simply being in it: Anne Jackson, Jennifer Suter, Brian & Jenni Clayville, Brent & Tam Hodge, David & Diane Goodwin, Brice Bohrer, Carlos & Heather Whittaker, Chad & Sarah Markley, Grant Mong, Jenny Miller, Jud & Lori Wilhite, Julie Jobe, Erin English, Francois Driessen, Dana Bowman, Darren & Charla Miley, Tal Prince, Larry & Tina Rutledge, Laura Lasky, Melanie McGaughey, Nicole Wick, Alece Ronzino, Jasmin Harrington, Andy Addis, Bernie Leslie, Brad Mann, Daniel Horning, Robert & Melissa Hingula, Amber Masters, Amber Pistole, Rebecca Simmons, Brenda McLellan, Jon Nelson, Kem Meyer, Luke Gilkerson, Lynse Stevens, Connie Horosz, Dan & Mary Southerland, Dan Chaverin, and Rindy Walton.

To the staff at Westside Family Church, I found my call to ministry under your leadership and care. Thank you for your generous support as I wrote this book. Particular thanks to Matt Adams who took a chance and hired me when I was only a nineteen-year-old kid, and Dick Dearwester and Barbara Bridges for giving me the opportunity to facilitate my first recovery groups. Without that experience, I might never have known I could do this ministry.

To AmyChristine, Charlotte, Chelsea, Jennifer, and Stephanie, for your bravery in sharing your story. Your sacrifice will inspire many more women to freedom.

Acknowledgments

To my fellow Dirty Girls, for how you inspire me every day to keeping doing this ministry. Know that you are not alone and that you, my sisters, were called to be free.

Thanks to Steve Lyon, Deb Keiser, and the whole team at Moody Publishers for believing in the message of this book.

And I want to thank Jesus. For how He continues to pull me out of the mire when the ground beneath me sinks, for how He trusts me with responsibilities I still don't feel adequate enough to possess, and for how He loves me even at the times when I love myself the least.

IT'S NEVER TOO LATE

We've spent a considerable amount of time together talking about coming clean. About making a fresh start in our lives. But the most important decision you will ever make is doing what's best for your eternal life.

We're not trapped by our pasts; a future with Jesus is a future of hope.

"For I know the plans I have for you," declares the Lord, "plans to prosper you and not to harm you, plans to give you hope and a future" (Jeremiah 29:11).

But if you've never made the decision to follow Jesus I want to give you the opportunity to do so today. If you are ready to commit yourself not only to a life free from pornography addiction, but a life surrendered to Jesus Christ, then take a quiet moment now and pray this prayer:

Dear God,
I admit that I am a sinner. I have done many things that don't please You. I have lived my life for myself and for that I am sorry. And I ask You to forgive me. I believe that You died on the cross for me, to save me. You did what I could not do for myself. I come to You now and ask You to take control of not only my addiction, but my whole life; I give it all to You. I know that I will never be perfect, but help me to live every day in a way that pleases You. I love You, Lord. Amen.

That's it! I welcome you into the fold of God and congratulate you on making this incredible decision. Now that you've done so, please surround yourself with others who share and support your commitment and your new values at church or in a Christ-centered support group.

For Free Resources or to join DGM web based support groups check out

DIRTYGIRLSMINISTRIES.COM

moodypublishers.com